OF ALL TRIBES

TRIBES

AMERICAN INDIANS AND ALCATRAZ

JOSEPH BRUCHAC

ABRAMS BOOKS FOR YOUNG READERS

NEW YORK

NOTE FROM THE AUTHOR

Most Indigenous Americans commonly refer to themselves as "Indians." Many people believe "Native American" is the preferred term to use, but that is not true. While the word "Indian" is the result of a geographical misunderstanding on the part of Europeans, it has been in common use for hundreds of years among our Indigenous peoples. When a Smithsonian museum devoted to the cultures and histories of the original inhabitants of America was founded in 1989, it was the consensus of Indigenous scholars, elders, tribal leaders, and historians that it should be called the National Museum of the American Indian. Indigenous Americans, while generally comfortable with the English word "Indian," prefer to be identified first by their own tribal nation, such as Lakota or Dine. There are hundreds of different Indigenous languages, each with its own name for itself (a name usually meaning something such as "the People"). However, when referring to the Indigenous peoples of this nation in general, no one tribal name could be used for all. Thus, we end up with Indian, and for these reasons and more, I interchange "Indian" with "Native American" throughout this narrative.

Caption for title page: Indians of All Tribes tipi on Alcatraz.

Cataloging-in-Publication Data has been applied for and may be obtained from the Library of Congress.

ISBN 978-1-4197-5719-8

Text © 2023 Joseph Bruchac
Book design by Heather Kelly
Edited by Howard W. Reeves

Printed and bound in China
10 9 8 7 6 5 4 3 2 1

Abrams® is a registered trademark of Harry N. Abrams, Inc.

ABRAMS The Art of Books
195 Broadway, New York, NY 10007
abramsbooks.com

A sign on Alcatraz has been altered from "United States Property" to "United Indian Property."

CONTENTS

Aerial view of Alcatraz island with
San Francisco in the background

PREFACE

On November 20, 1969, a group of ninety or more Native Americans composed of different tribes—most of them college students and young activists in their twenties—crossed San Francisco Bay under the cover of darkness. They called themselves the "Indians of All Tribes." Their objective was to occupy the abandoned prison on Alcatraz Island, a mile and a half across the treacherous waters.

The Indians of All Tribes was not the first Native group to land on Alcatraz and claim it. There had been three previous attempts. On March 8, 1964, five Dakota Sioux had invaded the "the Rock," as Alcatraz had been called by those incarcerated there when it was a federal prison. They were accompanied by a lawyer who explained to the U.S. government that their claim was based on the 1868 Treaty of Fort Laramie between the Lakota and the federal government. That treaty stated that surplus federal property could be legally claimed by the Indians. Though their claim was eventually denied, that 1868 treaty would be part of the rationale for the later Native American attempts to lay claim to "abandoned" federal lands, beginning with the bleak twenty-two-acre island that had sat unused since its infamous prison was closed in 1963.

On November 9, 1969, a small group of Indians of All Tribes activists had managed to convince the owner of a boat called the *Monte Cristo* to take them on what he was told would merely be a symbolic cruise around the island. But when they were completing a circle of Alcatraz and within a hundred yards of its shore, several of the young men on board jumped off to swim to the island, where they again proclaimed it as Indian land—before being escorted off by the Coast Guard.

Then, later the same night, an even smaller group of All Tribes activists landed on Alcatraz. There, they remained hidden through the night, using the opportunity to scout the island's resources and plan for their next attempt, which would be larger and geared toward occupation. In the morning, they too were escorted off the island.

The November 20, 1969, attempt, however, proved to be better organized, more widely supported, and much longer lived than any of its predecessors.

However, the story behind that attempt by the Indians of All Tribes begins long before that late November boat ride across the dark waters of San Francisco Bay. There's a history that needs to be told to bring that iconic island and the events that transpired there into clearer focus. It's a history that begins long before the turbulent 1960s. It includes decades of Indian policy crafted in Washington, D.C., including the 1832 Supreme Court's so-called Doctrine of Discovery, based on a papal bull in 1493 that justified the taking by Christian Europeans of the Indigenous lands of the entire western hemisphere.

Then there is the history of Alcatraz Island itself, a history that led it to be chosen as the site of the most infamous prison in America. It's with that history that we'll begin.

A contemporary illustration of how an Ohlone Village of Pruistac might have appeared in the mid-1700s

CHAPTER 1

OHLONE LAND

The Ohlone people of the San Francisco Bay Area, known today as the Muwekma Ohlone Tribe, are an organized Native nation that still exists and continues to assert its identity. They were, for a time, federally recognized and have struggled for more than two decades to regain that recognition. Recognition is a legal term meaning that the U.S. government recognizes a government-to-government relationship with an Indian tribe inside the borders of the United States. In most cases, those relationships are based on treaties signed between the United States and the tribe. One of the ironies of Native American life is that an Indian tribe does not legally "exist"—that is, enjoy some degree of self-government and control of its own land or qualify for certain federal or state benefits—until it has been recognized by either the federal or a state government.

Occupying most of the coast in and around present-day San Francisco as far south as Monterey, the Ohlone in the period before European colonization lived in as many as forty different villages along the shores of the bay, each a small, independent community. The eighteenth-century Spanish called them Costeños, people of the coast—a term that later became Costanoan. It's a name that the original Bay Area people and their descendants never accepted, preferring the word "Ohlone." That may have been the name of one of their larger villages. It also might mean "western people" in the language of a tribal nation to their east, the Miwok.

Those whose community was closest to Alcatraz Island were the Ramaytush branch of the Ohlone people. Although the Ramaytush would go to Alcatraz Island to hunt birds and gather the eggs from the nesting ground there, it seems that no one lived on the island then by choice. It's been said that one way the Ramaytush had of punishing offenders was to exile them to the island for a period of time. There, separated from the vital life of their people, someone who'd done something wrong would have time to contemplate how to fit back into the community.

A mile and a half offshore, surrounded by the strong currents of the wide San Francisco Bay, Alcatraz Island seems to many to have always been an uninviting place. Comprising only twenty-two acres, its highest elevation is 135 feet.

A Spanish explorer, Lieutenant Juan Manuel de Ayala, gave the island its name in 1775, dubbing it Isla de los Alcatraces, later Anglicized to Alcatraz. Translated as Island of the Pelicans, it refers to the large colony of pelicans and other seabirds that de Ayala observed on the island. Although it was and remains a nesting area for seabirds, Alcatraz is mostly rock and has never had much vegetation. For that reason, before the Spanish arrival, there seems to have been no permanent occupation by anyone, including the Ohlone.

———

Greg Castro, a contemporary member of the Ramaytush, offered an Indigenous perspective about Alcatraz's past in response to an inquiry about what its original name might have been.

OF ALL TRIBES

Although there is little doubt that the place now called "Alcatraz" was part of the Ramaytush Yelamu homeland [being just offshore a short distance from one of the known major long-term village sites], we have not found documentation that shares the name our ancestors had for that place. That is not surprising, because so far, we have only found about two-hundred-plus words of our language preserved in documentation of the initial colonizers' records, so many important words are still "asleep" to us.

I specifically used the term "place." I hope that people are aware that it was not always an "island." Within Ramaytush cultural presence, back several thousands of years ago, it was likely a hill, as it was in an area before the bay was created by rising sea level. We and other communities in the surrounding area could actually walk to "the island"! Back in ancient times, other communities, we believe, had some acknowledgment of the place as well—it probably "stuck out" prominently from the landscape of the time and so likely the Coast Miwok to the north and the Chochenyo to the east were aware of it. I have heard Corrina Could

(Chochenyo), Federated Villages of Lisjan, speak of the island as a "west-facing portal" to the West [Afterlife] for her people. I have never heard her mention the name before, if it is known.

———

Land, in the European sense of property ownership, was meant to be bought and sold, developed, and used commercially. This was not a concept shared by the many Indigenous first nations of the part of the continent now known as California. It is certainly true that individual Indigenous communities thought of the lands—and waters—of their homelands as theirs, to be taken care of and defended for future generations. But the buying and selling of that land was not something they could imagine. The land was and remains a living presence, a source of life as connected to a person as their human mother. How could someone sell their mother?

That question was often asked of colonizing Europeans throughout the continent as more and more Native lands passed out of Indigenous ownership—usually as a result of pressure, misunderstanding, forced resettlement, warfare, and direct attempts at cultural and physical genocide. The record of Europeans in California is particularly bad in that respect. First there was the period of European exploration from 1542 to 1769. Then came the colonial period under the Spanish, roughly from 1760 to 1821. When Mexico gained independence from Spain in 1821, California was part of the nation of Mexico. Then, after the Mexican-American War, which spanned from 1846 to 1848, it became a territory of the United States and in 1851 a state. In each of those periods, the Indigenous people of the region were described as subhuman. "Digger Indians," for example, was a derisive term that originated in the widespread Native practice of harvesting edible roots as part of a varied and quite nutritious diet. But the implication of "diggers" was that such behavior proved they were primitive, lacking any real culture, barely human. Under both Spanish and American rule, Indians often were hunted and killed, as if they were animals. In the words of the early nineteenth-century Franciscan friar Geronimo Boscana, "The Indians of California may be compared to a species of monkey."

One common myth is that the Indigenous peoples of the state were just "hunter-gatherers" and did not practice any kind of agriculture or land management. In fact, the continued management of ecosystems was part of precolonial Native life. Native Americans widely practiced the selective burning of brush to provide new growth for deer and other animals to feed upon—and also to prevent the kinds of devastating wildfires that have become common throughout California in the twenty-first century. Among the Ohlone, the Chumash, and numerous other groups, acorns, which were a staple food, were harvested in such large numbers that often enough could be stored to last two years. Early European visitors to the state remarked on how strange it was that the oak forests the Indians relied upon grew as if they were planted in rows. But that was not by chance. Many of those groves were indeed planted by Native people.

Further, Indigenous precolonial communities were universally careful about harvesting too much and killing too many of the terrestrial and maritime species that filled out their diets. As anthropologist Robert F. Heizer puts it, "California Indians were highly accomplished practical botanists and zoologists . . . knowledgeable in a different way, a way directed at understanding nature in such a manner as to use it without destroying it." There was also the widespread practice of planting a Native grain, half the size of wheat, along the coast and in major valleys. Rather than being plowed under, the fields would be burned after harvest and then the grain seed spread across the land.

It was only after the destruction of habitats and species by Europeans and the domestic animals they introduced— horses, cattle, goats, and sheep, which overgrazed the land— that California Indians were encountered by missionaries such as Father Junípero Serra "in a starving condition." At this point, they were herded into missions where they often continued to starve on the meager and inadequate rations they were allotted.

The Native population of the state diminished from an estimated four to five hundred thousand at the time of European arrival to less than fifty thousand by the start of the twentieth century. Much of that diminishment occurred during the time of the Spanish missions.

During the mission period, from 1769 to 1821, the Indigenous populations, including the Ohlone, were forced to leave their own villages and resettle at missions, where they were Christianized and used as an enslaved labor force. Father Serra (1713–1784) was canonized as a Catholic saint in 1988 for his benevolent work with the Native people of California. However, Serra never spoke out against the brutal treat-

A nineteenth-century drawing by Alexander F. Harmer of California Indians working at a Spanish mission

ment of his brown-skinned flock. In fact, he was the driving force behind the conquest and colonization of the state. He advocated corporal punishment of all kinds—whipping, shackles, sharpened prods—for recalcitrant Indians. On one occasion, a large number of Native children died in one of the plagues that became more common after *los Indios* were removed from their villages and crammed together in the missions. Serra rejoiced at their deaths, claiming a victory since they had been baptized before they died and thus their souls had been saved. Native people in California today point out that the bones of their ancestors may be found not only in unmarked graves but also in the walls of every Catholic mission in the state.

In the early years of Spanish rule, the same Alcatraz Island that had been used by the Raymatush as a place of exile was now sometimes a refuge for Ohlone people seeking to escape the harsh mission system.

According to Adam Fortunate Eagle (formerly Adam Nordwall), who is one of the major forces behind the takeover of Alcatraz, there was another Native tradition about the rocky island that was more foreboding. A longtime resident of the Bay Area himself, Fortunate Eagle notes in his book *Heart of the Rock*, written in collaboration with Tim Findley, the following about Annie Oakes, the wife of Richard Oakes, the most charismatic of the leaders of the takeover: "Among her own Pomo people the island was always said to have been cursed and avoided by others in the Costanoan tribes as a place of bad spirits. Annie hated the island, and she dreaded all the attention it was bringing to Richard."

CHAPTER 2

AN AMERICAN CONQUEST

The American stories of Alcatraz, of the state of California, and of the colonizing of the West are inextricably linked to an idea known as "Manifest Destiny," which characterized the vision that many (but not all) Americans had of the future of their new nation. Essentially, it meant that white American settlers were destined to expand across the North American West, to "tame" the land, and to remake it in the image of the East. Such expansion was tantamount to a mandate from God, an inevitability. America's greatest heroes throughout the period were explorers and pioneers, such as Lewis and Clark and Daniel Boone, and Indian fighters, such as George Armstrong Custer.

Manifest Destiny became the underlying policy of the U.S. government throughout the eighteenth and nineteenth centuries. Anything and anyone standing in the way of that sacred destiny was conquered, swept aside, or eliminated. That included the original owners and inhabitants of the land, the Native Americans, who were the primary opponents of that expansionist policy.

During the nineteenth century, despite the United States' wars with Britain, Spain, and Mexico, and even among its own states, the primary enemies of America remained Indians. In fact, the Indian Wars had gone on for centuries—since the 1500s, when the period of European warfare with the original peoples of the Americas began with the arrival of Spanish and English colonists—and ended only with the surrender of Geronimo, the Chiricahua Apache resistance fighter, in 1886. It was the longest period of warfare in American history.

———

Manifest Destiny's campaign of continental conquest also succeeded far sooner than many expected. President Thomas Jefferson, who purchased the vast Louisiana Territory from France in 1803 and sent the Lewis and Clark Corps of Discovery Expedition to explore the route to the Pacific, had assumed it would take centuries to settle the vast continent. But the United States managed to stretch "from sea to shining sea" within less than one hundred years.

The road to California's becoming part of the United States led through Mexico, beginning in a troubled part of that southern republic that had finally freed itself from Spanish rule in 1821 after a decade of war. It was the Mexican state then called Tejas.

After Mexico gained that independence from Spain, the new nation extended an invitation for settlers from the United States to come to Coahuila y Tejas, one of the constituent states formed under the Mexican constitution of 1824. Tejas was a sparsely populated area, compared to the central and southern areas of Mexico—at least as far as European settlers were concerned. There were, however, a number of Indigenous Native peoples already there, in particular the powerful Comanches, often called the Lords of the Plains. Those new English-speaking settlers, who quickly began calling themselves Texans, helped "tame" the state by dispossessing the Indians.

Unfortunately for Mexico, those new Texans then

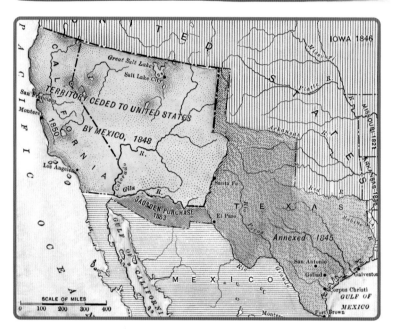

This map shows the area formerly part of Mexico that was ceded to the United States between 1848 and 1853, after the conclusion of the Mexican-American War. Texas, once a territory of Mexico, had already gained independence in 1836 and was annexed to the United States in 1845, influencing the onset of the war.

decided they wished to be independent of Mexican rule and revolted. That 1835 revolution, led by such men as Sam Houston, resulted in the creation of a new independent nation, the Republic of Texas, which lasted from March 1836 to February 1846.

During that decade, Mexico viewed Texas not as a country in its own right but as a rebellious province that would eventually be brought back into the fold. When the Republic of Texas finally asked to be admitted to the United States, a joint resolution of Congress agreed to its annexation. Then, on May 13, 1846, the United States declared war on Mexico. The unequal contest saw the capture of Mexico City in September 1847 and the signing of the Treaty of Guadalupe Hidalgo. The United States agreed to pay Mexico 15 million dollars in exchange for 55 percent of Mexican territory: five hundred thousand square miles. It included not just Texas but all Mexican claims to what is now Oklahoma, Utah, New Mexico, Arizona, Colorado, Wyoming, Montana, Washington, Oregon . . . and California.

With the defeat of Mexico, the era of American domination of the West truly began. And in every one of those present-day states, a new era of conflict with American Indian tribes also began whenever Indigenous people refused to see the land that sustained them as now belonging to something called the United States.

In early March 1847, Alcatraz Island was purchased for $5,000 by John C. Fremont. Fremont, a champion of

Manifest Destiny, had been appointed the military governor of California even before the defeat of Mexico. Viewing the island as a place from which to defend the Bay Area, he made the purchase in the name of the United States. Although Fremont was never reimbursed, the U.S. government eventually took control of the island. Because of the huge gold deposits then being found in the state, the U.S. government decided that San Francisco, where much of that mineral wealth was being taken, needed protection. A ring of fortifications on and around the bay was designed with Alcatraz as a key point, set aside as a military reservation in 1850 under an executive order from President Millard Fillmore. Government on the formerly undeveloped island began soon after. In 1853, the first lighthouse on the California coast was erected, featuring a lens imported from France. By 1858, the first fort on the island was completed, with one hundred cannons and a garrison of two hundred soldiers.

Because it was isolated from the mainland by the cold waters of the bay, whose currents were so swift that it was thought no swimmer could survive them, Fort Alcatraz began to accept military prisoners soon after its completion. Many of its inmates during the years of the American Civil

A nineteenth-century illustration of prospectors panning for gold during the California Gold Rush

War (1861–1865) were Confederate sympathizers and other Americans accused of treason, although it also was still a military fortress. It was not until 1907, when it became clear that forts were no longer needed to protect San Francisco, that it became solely a military prison.

Although Alcatraz had been used to house prisoners during its time as a military fort, the construction of the formal prison took place in stages, beginning in 1863. The cells of what became known as the "lower prison" were constructed first. They were dark, dank, and barely large enough for a man to turn around in. Much of the construction of the later parts of the prison, as well as the leveling of the islands' peaks to create a flat area on top, was done by prisoners. Even the shape of the island was changed as rocks and dirt were dumped into the bay, actually increasing the island's size. Barracks, a hospital, officer's quarters, and other structures were gradually added, making the island a small city unto itself.

The start of the twentieth century saw the construction of the second structure to house inmate cells, a wooden building known as the "upper prison." By 1904, it had completely replaced the lower prison. Accommodating 307 prisoners, the cells of the new prison were roomier, safer, and, though still spartan, provided more amenities.

Finally, in 1912, a new, larger concrete prison was built.

Designed by Colonel Reuben Turner, who had been the prison commandant, it is the legendary building that stands on the island to this day. It was, at the time, the largest concrete structure in the world and was equipped with electricity and steam heating. Its imposing mass—five hundred feet long and consisting of three tiers of cells—is broken up into four separate cellblocks with a holding capacity of six hundred prisoners.

It's easy to imagine, even today, when you approach the island, just how foreboding that barren place must have appeared to any man sentenced to life on the Rock as he saw it from a prison launch rising out of the fog. Yet, for a few brief months, the island was seen as something else by the Native Americans and their supporters who occupied it—a place of promise, the symbol of a better future.

FRANK LESLIE'S

ILLUSTRATED

NEWSPAPER

Entered according to the Act of Congress, in the year 1873, by Frank Leslie, in the office of the Librarian of Congress, at Washington.

No. 928—Vol. XXXVI.] NEW YORK, JULY 12, 1873. [Price, with Supplement, 10 Cents.

BOSTON CHARLEY, MURDERER OF REV. DR. THOMAS.

SHACK NASTY JIM.

HOOKER JIM, THE OPPONENT OF MR. DWYER.

SCAR-FACED CHARLEY, THE FRIEND OF STEELE.

DONALD M'KAY, THE HALF-BRED WARM SPRING SCOUT WHO TRAILED THE MODOCS.

CAPTAIN JACK.

ONE-EYED DIXIE, THE SQUAW INTERPRETER.

SCHONCHIN, WHO TRIED TO MURDER MEACHAM.

STEAMBOAT FRANK, GEN. DAVIS'S GUIDE.

CURLY-HEADED DOCTOR, THE MODOC MEDICINE MAN.

BOGUS CHARLEY, THE MODOC

THE MODOC INDIANS.—FROM PHOTOGRAPHS BY C. F. WATKINS, SAN FRANCISCO.—SEE PAGE 287.

Front page of Frank Leslie's *Illustrated Newspaper* with portraits of eleven prisoners. Several Modoc War veterans were imprisoned at Alcatraz.

CHAPTER 3

EXILED TO ALCATRAZ

I f the Island of the Pelicans had been a place of refuge for local Native people during the time of the Spanish rule, for some American Indians it became the opposite in the late nineteenth and early twentieth centuries. They ended up there as federal prisoners. "From 1873 to 1895, thirty-two Native Americans from various tribes were imprisoned on Alcatraz."

The reason for this was solely a result of government Indian policy. The U.S. policy of dealing with the "Indian Problem" had transitioned in the last quarter of the nineteenth century from outright warfare to two policies that today would be deemed cultural genocide. The first of these was an accelerated taking of tribal lands throughout the continent by treaty, forced sale, or outright theft or by removing entire nations of Native people from their homelands—a policy in place since the Indian Removal Act of 1830. Native people were then confined to reservations where they were little more than prisoners, not allowed to leave their boundaries without a pass or permission from an Indian agent appointed by the U.S. government.

Some of those who resisted those mandates ended up at Alcatraz. The first, on June 5, 1873, was Paiute Jim. After he was transferred from Camp McDermit in Nevada, his stay on the island was the shortest on record. Two days after his arrival, he was shot and killed by a guard. The next two Indian prisoners were veterans of the Modoc War, fought in southern Oregon when 150 Modocs led by Kintpuash (Captain Jack) left the Klamath Reservation in 1872 and returned to a part of what had been their original homeland. They did so because life on the crowded reservation—away from their traditional sources of food and livelihood in general—was so hard for them. For a time things went well, but eventually the army attempted to move them back to the reservation. They then took refuge in the lava beds of Tule Lake, where they resisted for months the several armies sent against them. When they finally surrendered, on June 4, 1873, the so-called ringleaders were sentenced to death. Kintpuash and three others were hanged—their heads cut off and sent to the Army Medical Museum. President Ulysses Grant commuted the death sentences of the other two, Barncho and Sloluck, to life imprisonment on Alcatraz. On May 28, 1875, Barncho died of scrofula, a form of tuberculosis. Sloluck remained a prisoner on Alcatraz until February 1878, when he was sent to Fort Leavenworth and later allowed to join the rest of his exiled people in Indian Territory.

From 1874 to 1887, the Indians sentenced to Alcatraz also included Paiutes, Chiricahua, and San Carlos Apaches, and in 1894, the largest group of Native Americans arrived on the island: nineteen "Moqui hostiles." The crimes committed by these men, all members of the Hopi Nation, were in large part a direct result of the second policy of cultural genocide instituted by the United States in the nineteenth century—Indian boarding schools.

Hopi Prisoners at Alcatraz Prison in 1894

OF ALL TRIBES

Beginning with the creation of the Carlisle Indian Industrial School in 1879, vast numbers of Native American children from throughout the continent were taken from their families and communities and forced to go to distant church- and government-run institutions. During the thirty years of Carlisle's existence, more than twelve thousand attended the school. Hundreds of such schools were established, and there the Indigenous students were made to speak only English, were subjected to harsh military discipline, often were poorly fed and abused, and were ravaged by such diseases as tuberculosis. The stated intention was to "kill the Indian and save the man." In many of those schools—and similar institutions in Canada—large numbers of Indian children actually did die.

The policy of forcing Native children to attend those schools was resisted by some Native communities. None were more resistant than the Hopi people. Hopis have long described themselves as a people of peace—with no tradition of warring against other tribal nations or white people. But the majority of Hopis resisted the government policy of sending their children to schools where they were beaten if they spoke Hopi or engaged in any form of non-Christian religious practice. Those Hopis in the community opposed to the boarding school—and the breaking up of their communal farms into individual allotments—became known to the government as "hostiles." Attempts to enforce allotment and attendance at the dismal, crowded Keams Canyon School were met by passive resistance.

On November 25, 1894, troops were sent onto the "Moqui" Indian Agency to the village of Orayvi to arrest the so-called ringleaders. Nineteen Hopi men were sent to Fort Wingate and then on to Alcatraz. There they were to "be held in confinement, at hard labor, until they shall show they fully realize the error of their evil ways until they shall evince, in an unmistakable manner, a desire to cease interference with the plans of the government for the civilization and education of its Indian wards."

Their stay on the island began on January 3, 1895. Housed in the Lower Prison, with its cramped, damp cells and poor ventilation, they rose early and worked each day. These were the last Native American inmates to be sent as prisoners of war to Alcatraz; their incarceration ended on August 7, 1895, and they were allowed to return home after promises to obey all orders.

However, as Matthew Saskiestewa Gibert put it in his book *Hopi Runners*, "the U.S. government's attempt to 'restructure' the minds of Hopi people did not go unchallenged." In 1907, another group of Hopi men from the village of Songoopavi on Second Mesa were arrested for opposing the government policy of forcing Hopi children to attend Indian Schools. Described as "hostiles," they were taken to Fort Defiance in Arizona. From there, rather than Alcatraz, even though they were all grown men, they were sent to a government school much more distant than the one they had opposed—the United States Indian Industrial School in Carlisle, Pennsylvania, more than two thousand miles away. One of those young men, who gained unexpected fame, was Louis Tewanima.

Running is a sacred thing among the Hopi. It's also often a matter-of-fact part of everyday life. As teenagers, Louis Tewanima and his friends would run in the morning to watch the train go by on the tracks fifty miles away from their community and then run back home in the afternoon.

One of the first things he did when he got to the Carlisle Indian Industrial School in Pennsylvania was to run away. He and another young Hopi man managed to get as far as Texas. There, they were arrested by a local sheriff and sent by train back to Carlisle.

The head coach for the Carlisle track team was a man whose name would become famous in the annals of American football: Pop Warner. His Carlisle Indian team, featuring the great running back Jim Thorpe, would defeat all of the powerhouse schools of their time—even though Carlisle Indian Industrial School only went from kindergarten through high school and was not a college like their opponents. The entire enrollment of Carlisle was never more than one thousand people, many of whom were quite young.

Pop Warner also prided himself on his track team. One day, after their failed attempt to escape, Louis and the other Hopi prisoners came to Pop Warner's track practice. In rudimentary English, Louis said something like "We Hopis run fast good." Since Louis was small and skinny, with legs like pipe cleaners, Warner was skeptical, but he told them to start running. When they were still running half an hour later, he realized that he was onto something.

OF ALL TRIBES

Warner's Carlisle Indian Industrial School track team, featuring Louis Tewanima, would dominate college athletics. Louis was selected to go to the Olympic games twice and in 1912 won a silver medal in the 10,000 meters.

Ironically, Louis was not a U.S. citizen then. In fact, Louis Tewaniuma (who might, thirteen years earlier, have ended up at Alcatraz for resisting a government school) was still a prisoner of war at a government school when he represented the United States of America.

A month after his return from the Olympics in 1912, Tewanima was finally allowed to return home to the Hopi mesas. He gave away his medals to his peers at Carlisle and lived out the rest of his long life in Songoopavi as a respected elder in the Antelope Society.

At the same 1912 Olympics, another Native American young man accomplished a feat even greater than that of Tewanima. Jim Thorpe, a Sac and Fox from Oklahoma and also a student at Carlisle, would win both the decathlon and the pentathlon. But Jim did not get to keep his gold medals. When a reporter revealed that Jim had played semi-pro baseball for two summers prior to 1912, he was stripped of his Olympic titles. In those days, to be in the Olympics, you had to be a complete amateur and not have been paid in any way for athletic competition. It was far different from the modern era, when famous professional athletes regularly go to the Olympics and represent their nations. Jim's earnings playing "summer ball" were laughably small. It was common practice for college athletes to go into the Carolina league during the summers, although most played under assumed names. In fact, Pop Warner, Jim's football coach at Carlisle, had encouraged Jim and other Carlisle athletes to play in the summer leagues to stay in shape and earn a little spending money.

Rather than defending Jim, Pop Warner (to protect his own reputation) had him sign a letter (written for him by Warner) confessing that he had played summer ball without knowing it was wrong because he was an "ignorant Indian." And it was Warner who insisted on Jim returning his trophies.

Although Jim's long career as an athlete, spanning many sports, would be a thing of legend and he was arguably the most famous Native American of his time, Thorpe did not live to see the return of his medals. He passed on in 1953, sixteen years before the Alcatraz Indian takeover. But in an interesting turn of fate, the injustice he suffered would become a part of the Indian story of Alcatraz when his daughter Grace would join the Alcatraz takeover.

CHAPTER 4

TWENTY-NINE YEARS AS THE LAST STOP

In 1933, the military ended its relationship with Alcatraz. Jurisdiction over the island was transferred to the Federal Bureau of Prisons, which remained in control of Alcatraz until the prison's final closure in 1963.

New gates and steel bars were installed, and six guard towers were built. It had become what was felt to be the most escape-proof prison in America, truly modern and designed to hold the worst federal prisoners. With the island located a mile and a half from the mainland, only government ships were allowed to land. Civilian craft had to remain at least two hundred yards offshore.

Despite its high levels of security, there would be

OF ALL TRIBES

fourteen escape attempts over the twenty-nine years of Alcatraz's existence as a federal prison. Of the thirty-six men who attempted to escape, two were found drowned, six were shot and killed, and all the others—with five notable exceptions—were caught before leaving the island and returned to their cells.

Though life was spartan, the prison did offer some services to its inmates. The library on Alcatraz held fifteen thousand books. In those days before television or cell phones, the library was one of the most popular parts of the prison for the inmate population. The average inmate read between seventy-five and one hundred books a year, and working in the prison library was one of the best jobs an inmate could have.

There was a prison barbershop. The inmate barbers even had access to scissors and razors. James Lucas, one of the prison barbers, once held a pair of scissors to the throat of notorious gangster Al Capone when he tried to cut in line. Capone, public enemy number one, inmate #83, was among the most famous of the Alcatraz inmates. Ironically, while on the island, he was well behaved. He even belonged to the prison band, the Rock Islanders, playing the banjo. "Big Al" was known to be a "rat," an informant for the guards. That reputation resulted in his being stabbed in the back with a pair of scissors by the same James Lucas who had threatened him before. Capone spent a month in the hospital as a result of that attack—one of several attempts on his life. His time on the Rock lasted until January 6, 1939.

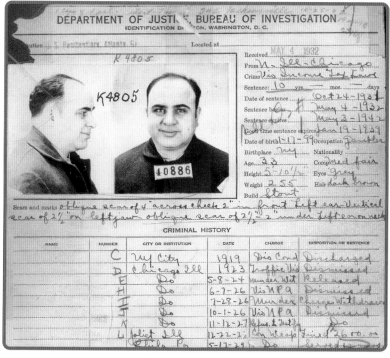

Al Capone's criminal arrest record from the Department of Justice Bureau of Investigations, 1932

The two most famous escape attempts from Alcatraz involved a Native American man named Clarence Carnes, often called "the Choctaw Kid."

Just eighteen when he arrived, Clarence Carnes was the youngest convict ever sent to Alcatraz. An Oklahoma Choctaw, he was a direct descendent of great-grandparents who had been sent on the Trail of Tears from their southern homeland in Mississippi to Indian Territory. Born on Choctaw Nation land in Billy, Oklahoma, Carnes grew up in poverty. After a number of petty crimes, including stealing candy bars from his school when he was a child, in 1943, he became involved in an attempted holdup that ended in a garage attendant's death. Though he may not have been the one who did it, he was convicted for the murder and sentenced to life in prison at the age of sixteen and sent to Oklahoma Granite Reformatory.

Prison is never easy to accept for Native Americans—whose traditional cultures generally put an emphasis on personal freedom and continued interaction with the natural world—and Clarence Carnes was no exception. Two years after his life sentence, he and a number of other inmates engineered an escape from the reformatory. After being caught, another ninety-nine years was added onto his sentence—for kidnapping a hostage taken while he and the other escapees were on the run.

Seen now as an escape risk, Carnes was sent to Leavenworth Prison in Kansas, a maximum-security facility. There, he also almost succeeded in another attempt to break out. Known now as the "Choctaw Kid," escape-proof Alcatraz was the next logical step for him. At Alcatraz, he was examined by a prison psychiatrist, who diagnosed his desire for freedom as a result of a "psychopathic personality." He was, the psychiatrist said, "emotionally unstable." Because he scored only a 93 on an IQ test (a test that, because of their unfamiliarity with Western cultural norms, Indians seldom did well on), Carnes was declared to be of below average intelligence.

But the Rock did not discourage him for trying again to gain his freedom. He arrived on Alcatraz on July 6, 1945. Ten months later, on May 2, 1946, he and five other inmates attempted one of the most famous prison escape attempts in American history. Those six men managed to make their way out of their cells. But even though they'd managed to get weapons, they were stopped before they could leave the concrete prison. They refused to surrender or give up the guards they'd taken as hostages. The fierce gunfight that followed—the

Ringleaders of Alcatraz Escape Attempts of 1946. From left: Marvin Hubbard, Bernard Paul Coy, and Clarence Carnes.

infamous "Battle of Alcatraz"—resulted in the death of two prison officers and three inmates during the escape attempt.

Despite having been sentenced for murder, Clarence Carnes was not a killer. He refused the orders of the leader of his fellow escapees to take the lives of prison guards being held hostage. He and the other two surviving inmates actually went back to their cells and took no part in the gun battle that lasted two full days between the prison guards and the three inmates determined to die fighting. They finally got their wish after reinforcements were brought in that included U.S. Marines on their way back from Okinawa, Japan, where they had been stationed during World War II. At one point, a naval vessel was brought in to shell the cellblock.

Carnes's treatment of those hostages—which saved their lives—resulted in their testifying on his behalf during the later trial. While the other two surviving inmates were sentenced to death and eventually executed in the gas chamber at San Quentin State Prison, Carnes simply had ninety-nine more years added to his sentence, making it life plus another 203 years.

The Choctaw Kid may have been the most likable person incarcerated on the Rock. Other inmates all spoke well of him. For a number of years, he was confined to a cell next to the one occupied by Robert Stroud. Stroud became famous as the "Birdman of Alcatraz" for writing books about the diseases of canaries. (His life, heavily reimagined, became a major motion picture in 1962, with Burt Lancaster cast as Stroud.) Stroud taught Carnes to play chess. Despite his supposedly "below average" intelligence, Carnes became the best chess player on Alcatraz. Stroud also donated some of the royalties from his book *Digest of Bird Diseases* to a defense fund for his Indian friend. Carnes also made friends with the well-known, powerful Boston organized crime figure James "Whitey" Bulger, whose brother was a respected Massachusetts state senator.

Among his many other inmate friends were two brothers, John and Clarence Anglin. By then, Carnes was working in the prison library. No inmate was more closely watched by the guards than Carnes, due to his record. So, when the brothers began plotting an attempt to get off the Rock, he didn't try to join them. But he provided advice and helpful information to the Anglins and the two other convicts planning a daring escape. For example, he gave them an article from *Sports Illustrated* on how to make life rafts out of rubber raincoats. And, according to a later interview with Clarence, the night of the actual escape, he knew what was happening.

Although the official story was that the three men drowned in the waters of the bay (the fourth had not succeeded in joining them)—after digging through the crumbling concrete walls of their cells, climbing through roof vents, and then making it over the fences—their bodies were never found. They were pronounced dead due to the "impassable" nature of the waters of San Francisco Bay. However, three days after they went missing, the warden of Alcatraz received an unsigned post card. "Ha we made it!" is what it read. Carnes claimed that he had also received a postcard from those three men: Frank Maurice, John Anglin, and Clarence Anglin. It simply read "gone fishing," code words to let him know their escape succeeded. The three men were never apprehended.

Clarence Carnes visiting his
old cell in Alcatraz in 1980

OF ALL TRIBES

In 1963, four months before Alcatraz was closed, Clarence Carnes, the last Indian imprisoned on the Rock, was transferred to Springfield and then to the Leavenworth penitentiary. Despite the fact that his sentence was so incredibly long, he was eventually granted parole in October 1970 and allowed to go home to Oklahoma. For a time, he lived free, first in Oklahoma and then around Kansas City. He also traveled to visit his family in San Francisco. On at least one occasion, he visited Alcatraz, now a part of the National Park Service, sat in his old cell, and talked about his experiences there. But it was not easy to adjust to a life he hadn't known for more than forty years. He had drinking problems and was returned to prison for violating his parole. When he died in Missouri on October 5, 1988, he was a month away from being released again. He was buried in a pauper's grave.

But his past kindness to his fellow inmates was not forgotten. Less than a year later, Whitey Bulger, now free, purchased a $4,000 bronze coffin for his old friend. He had the Choctaw Kid's body exhumed and then paid for a car to transport his remains from Missouri back to Oklahoma. He was buried at the Billy cemetery in Daisy, Oklahoma, on Choctaw Nation land.

CHAPTER 5

CENTURIES OF DISHONOR

It has been said that the longest war in the history of the United States was waged in Afghanistan, but that is not true. The longest war was fought on American soil. That war, against the Native Americans of this continent, began centuries before the United States existed, soon after the first English colony was established at Jamestown, in 1607. As the boundaries of the new nation moved farther west, warfare against the original inhabitants of this land continued. The period of armed conflict lasted more than three centuries and did not end until the surrender of the last so-called renegade, Geronimo, and his Chiricahua Apaches in 1886.

But out-and-out warfare was not the only means used to separate Native people from land that European settlers wanted. More often than not, this separation was achieved via treaties—signed agreements between the United States and the various Native nations. Those treaties always resulted in the cession of more and more land to the ever-expanding United States. A total of 370 treaties were signed between 1778 and 1871. Without exception, every one of those treaties was broken by the United States.

The basic goal was Indian removal by any means possible. In 1830, the Indian Removal Act was signed, which required the Native nations of the American South—the so-called Five Civilized Tribes: the Cherokee, Choctaw, Chickasaw, Creek, and Seminole—to leave their land and move west to the area now known as Arkansas and Oklahoma, a territory that was supposed to be Indian land forever. It's been estimated that one hundred thousand Native people were relocated from such southern states as Georgia, Tennessee, North Carolina, South Carolina, Alabama, and Florida to Indian Territory, and that more than fifteen thousand died along the way.

Those Five Tribes were not the only ones affected. The

removal policy, which continued throughout much of the nineteenth century, had begun more than a century earlier, with the displacement of most of the tribal nations of the Northeast. Dozens of tribal nations were moved to the West, with the largest number going to Indian Territory. Today, of the thirty-nine Indian tribal nations in Oklahoma, only five are indigenous to that area.

But even that "Indian land forever" was not safe.

———

The Dawes Act of 1887 produced something called the "allot-ment policy." It ordered that land would no longer be held in common by tribal nations but would be divided up, with no more than 160 acres going to each tribal member. That left the majority of tribal lands declared as surplus. It was then made available to white settlers. The result was the Oklahoma land rush in 1889, the first of seven "land runs" into unassigned Indian lands. Thousands of land-hungry homesteaders lined up to stampede into the former Creek, Cherokee, Choctaw, Chickasaw, and Seminole reservations. Those settlers who "jumped the gun," sneaking in to stake out their claims before the official starting time, became known as "sooners," because they got there sooner. Ninety million acres were stripped from Native Americans, to be sold or allotted to non-Indian settlers.

The nineteenth century also produced an approach to solving America's "Indian problem" that was as devastating as the loss of tribal lands: taking Native American children from their families and sending them to government boarding schools. This was the same policy that the Hopi boys and men sent to Alcatraz had tried to oppose.

That policy was the indirect result of the Red River War of 1874. A coalition of Southern Plains tribes had sought to drive out the American buffalo hunters. After their defeat, a group of several dozen Native American combatants were sent as prisoners of war to Fort Marion in Florida. The officer in charge of them, Captain Richard Pratt, was remarkably forward-thinking for his time. He appeared to lack the common racial prejudice of many of his peers. George Armstrong Custer, for example, during the Civil War, had refused a command with Black soldiers, and his wife, Elizabeth, supposedly said she would shoot any Black soldier she saw approaching her door. In the war, Pratt had served well and without complaint as one of the all-white officers in charge of the 10th Cavalry, the Black servicemen who became popularly known as Buffalo Soldiers. Pratt believed that a Black man could be the equal in uniform of a white man and extended that belief to his Indian POWs.

At Fort Marion, he embarked on an unusual experiment. He dressed his young Native charges in military uniforms, gave them classes in English and Bible studies, and drilled them like soldiers. His success was memorable.

Lieutenant Richard Henry Pratt, founder and superintendent of Carlisle Indian School, 1879

Almost without exception, his Native American prisoners were exemplary students and appeared to have become "civilized." Several of those men actually went on to become Christian ministers.

Using them as examples of his approach, Pratt proposed to the government that educating Native children was the best way to solve the Indian problem. By sending Indigenous children to boarding schools, rebelliousness would be educated out of them. The aim would be to "kill the Indian and save the man."

Students of Carlisle Indian School, circa 1884

Pratt's proposal received the blessing of the government, and he went on to found the famous U.S. Carlisle Indian Industrial School in Carlisle, Pennsylvania.

Similar schools sprang up all around the country. Between 1860 and 1978, 367 Indian boarding schools operated in the United States. Over 150,000 Indian children attended them over those 118 years. There, the children had their hair cut short, were dressed in uniforms, were subjected to military discipline, and were forbidden to speak their languages or engage in any traditional practices. It was common for children to try to run away, only to be caught and returned, although some died while attempting to escape— freezing in the winter or struck by trains as they followed the tracks they hoped would lead them home.

To be fair, not all Indian boarding schools were the same. Some Native people managed to gain an education at those institutions, which enabled them to lead better lives. The conditions found on some reservations were worse than those in the schools where they were sent. Adam Fortunate Eagle told me in an interview that the fifteen years he spent first in the Pipestone Indian Training School and then at Haskell Institute were "the best thing that ever happened to me in my developing years. What I learned there gave me the knowledge and skills to have a successful career." Other prominent Native people, especially those who attended boarding schools after the 1920s, sometimes described the schools they attended as "their Harvard and Yale."

It is also true that boarding schools had consequences that were unintended and unforeseen by the government. Some students refused to lose their languages—such as the Navajo men who were later asked by the U.S. government to use their Native tongue to create an unbreakable code for sending radio messages during World War II. Those Navajo Code Talkers had spoken their languages in secret with each other when their white teachers could not hear them. Strong ties—and even marriages—between Indians from different tribes often developed as a result of people meeting in boarding schools. Indians from all across the country discovered how much they had in common, especially in terms of their desire for Native rights and the return of their lands. That intertribal realization of their oneness became known as the Pan-Indian Movement. One prominent result of that movement was the creation by boarding school alumni of the Native-led advocacy group known as the National Council of American Indians in 1926.

Even the better Indian boarding schools could be hotbeds of disease. Tuberculosis and flus often swept through those institutions. Some boarding school graveyards were filled with children who would never see their beloved families again. Sometimes Native students, especially in the Canadian Indian residential schools modeled on the U.S. system, simply disappeared. In Canada, decades after those schools were closed, it turned out that the rumors—repeated again and again by survivors of those institutions—of children being killed and secretly buried were true. In June 2021, the remains of 215 Indigenous children were found in a mass grave behind the Kamloops Indian Residential School in British Columbia.

During the century and more of their existence, Indian boarding schools in the United States and the similar residential schools in Canada affected virtually every Native American family in both countries as, generation after generation, their children were taken from them.

In her 1881 book, *A Century of Dishonor*, a survey of American Indian policy during the 1800s, Helen Hunt Jackson condemned virtually every aspect of the nation's dealings with Native Americans. The voices of Hunt and other white reformers were heard, and changes began in the first half of the twentieth century.

In 1924, Congress passed the Indian Citizenship Act, which granted full citizenship to all Native Americans. In 1928, the Meriam Report described the terrible conditions on Indian reservations and in most Indian boarding schools. When Franklin Delano Roosevelt came into office in 1932, his New Deal attempted to provide opportunities for Indians. John Collier, known for his insightful writing about Native history and culture, became the head of the Bureau of Indian Affairs (BIA) and put in place a number of groundbreaking reforms. These included support for tribal rights and encouraging Native arts and crafts. Some boarding schools became markedly better. More useful skills and trades were introduced, and certain aspects of Native culture were taught—especially the arts and crafts that Collier admired. The Indian Reorganization Act, passed by Congress in 1934 (the same year Alcatraz became a federal prison) and designed to improve life for Indians, returned limited rights of self-governance to tribal nations.

Some of the changes, though, were wrongheaded. Few were made with enough input from Native Americans. As a result, certain policies were either poorly enforced, inadequate, or just as bad for Native Americans as the practices of the years before. Although tribes were now given the right to limited self-governance, it was through the American democratic model of one man, one vote. This was a deep departure from ancient practices of governing by consensus—making sure everyone agreed with the decisions and laws made. Often only a few tribal members would vote in the elections, and traditional leaders were not represented. Another example of a reform that was meant to "help" Indians but was insultingly inadequate was the Indian Claims Commission, created by Congress in 1946. It was supposed to settle historic disputes over broken treaties. However, the amount proposed to reimburse tribes for land illegally taken from them was determined according to the value of that land when it was stolen. In the case of land taken from the California tribes, that amounted to forty-seven cents per acre.

Further Indian legislation passed in the 1950s brought no benefit and proved deeply harmful to Indians. The worst example was the Termination Policy of 1953, Public Law 280, which ordered many American Indian tribes to disband.

Then, after dividing part of their territories among individual tribal members, the bulk of their lands was sold. Between 1953 and 1964, 109 tribes and bands were terminated as sovereign independent nations. The U.S. government's reasoning behind this move was that Indians were being held back by their lands being communally held. They would do better as individual landowners like other Americans.

That assumption was deeply false. Deprived of most of their lands, formerly prosperous tribes such as the Menominee and the Klamath suffered deeply. Individual tribal members often had to sell the acreage they had been allocated to meet the taxes they were now required to pay each year.

The termination policy was followed by the BIA's Indian Relocation Act in 1956. It created the practice of encouraging Native people to leave their reservation communities and settle in a number of selected urban centers. There, they were promised training and meaningful employment. Given one-way tickets to Chicago, Denver, Seattle, Los Angeles, and other large urban centers, many of those relocated Indians discovered their housing to be substandard, the training inadequate, and the promised jobs nonexistent. Homelessness, joblessness, and culture shock were common experiences, and ghettoes of impoverished Indians sprang up in those relocation cities.

Many of those discouraged relocatees made their way back to their own communities, hitching rides, hopping freight trains, or just walking. This was the same period when America was starting its space program. One of the jokes in the Native community at the time was that the United States could save a lot of money if they used Indians as astronauts: "Just send an Indian one-way to the moon," the joke went. "Tell him it's relocation and he'll find his own way back."

By 1958, eight additional cities had been designated as sites for new relocation centers. Three of them were in California: Los Angeles, San Jose, and Oakland, which is right next to San Francisco. Although the program was voluntary, by the time someone reached the point of considering relocation, there was little about it that felt voluntary or, in most cases, positive. After being given that one-way bus ticket to the city they chose, those on relocation had to report every day to the relocation office to see if jobs were available. In most cases, they were not. Although social assistance for families was often provided, if you failed to report to the office every day, all the aid for your family would be cut off.

That social assistance also ended after the first paycheck, even though most jobs were temporary.

The most visible result of the relocation program was not opportunity but the creation of miniature reservations within those urban centers—Indian mini-cities made up not of one tribal nation but dozens. In those Indigenous ghettos, always in the poorest parts of a city, people fell into despair and alcoholism in large numbers.

The Bureau of Indian Affairs estimated that between 1958 and 1968, two hundred thousand Indians were moved to urban areas. That kind of mass removal of Natives had not taken place since the Indian Removal Act had emptied the South of the majority of its original people.

———

Further, many of those who ended up in those city ghettos were Native people whose reservations no longer existed. By 1969, a total of 109 reservations, rancherias, and Indian bands had been officially terminated.

While strides were being made toward securing justice for African Americans in the 1960s, Native Americans were largely left out. In fact, the landmark 1964 Civil Rights Act specifically excluded Indians.

OF ALL TRIBES

In some cases, one government agency seemed to be at odds with the other when it came to Native Americans and Indian policy in general. The Office of Economic Opportunity was supposedly concerned with reducing poverty on reservations. However, that did not align with the BIA policies of relocation and termination being implemented at the same time. What was offered by one hand of the government was taken away by the other hand.

It is little wonder that Indians tended to turn not toward but away from the U.S. government. By the 1960s, many intertribal movements were a growing factor in the lives of Native Americans. There was, for example, the activist National Indian Youth Council, formed in 1961 in Chicago by Mel Thom (Walker River Paiute) and Clyde Warrior (Ponca). This kind of political organizing had started much earlier, with such intertribal organizations as the previously mentioned National Council of American Indians, created in 1926 primarily by the Lakota author Zitkala-Sa (Gertrude Bonnin), and the National Congress of American Indians, founded in 1944. Both organizations were formed to advocate for Native rights and representation. One of the major goals of the National Congress had been to prevent the

INTERTRIBAL FRIENDSHIP HOUSE
OPEN WED. thru SUN. 2 to 10:30 P.M.

Sarah Brown
(Pomo) with her
niece Tina and her
nephew Anthony
Fourkiller at
Intertribal Friendship
House, Oakland, CA

end of the special wardship relation between tribal nations and the federal government that became known as termination. Although they had failed thus far to change the many destructive government policies affecting Native people, those national organizations and others continued to advocate for Indians.

In the San Francisco Bay Area, there were, by 1969, a number of local organizations advocating for Native Americans. The American Friends, the San Francisco Indian Council, the United Bay Area Council, the Intertribal Friendship House, and other tribal clubs were all involved in trying to make things better for local Native Americans.

However, the new generation of Native activists coming of age in the 1960s felt a different approach was needed. The work done by the older organizations had largely been behind the scenes, not before the eyes of the public. The first place where Indian intertribalism and its goals would become obvious to the wider world was in Alcatraz, with the takeover in 1969.

Although many relocated Indians returned to their reservations, going "back to the blanket," many others stayed in their new cities. Sizable pan-Indian communities that exist to this day developed in all of the cities the government had set up as relocation centers. Indeed, the U.S. Office of Minority Health estimated that as of May 21, 2021, only 22 percent of American Indians and Alaska Natives lived on reservations or other trust lands, while 60 percent resided in metropolitan areas.

As the flow of Native Americans into urban centers continued, one of the designated relocation areas with a substantial and growing Indian population was Oakland, California. By 1969, as many as forty thousand Native people—from dozens of different tribes—were living in Oakland, San Francisco, and the surrounding Bay Area. There, whenever the fog lifted, the abandoned island of Alcatraz was one of the most striking things those displaced Native Americans saw.

Articles of a Treaty made and concluded by and between Lieutenant General William T. Sherman, General William S. Harney, General Alfred H. Terry, General C. C. Augur, J. B. Henderson, Nathaniel G. Taylor, John B. Sanborn and Samuel F. Tappan, duly appointed Commissioners on the part of the United States and the different Bands of the Sioux Nation of Indians by their Chiefs and Head men whose names are hereto subscribed, they being duly authorized to act in the premises

Article I

From this day forward all war between the parties to this agreement shall forever cease. The Government of the United States desires peace and its honor is hereby pledged to keep it. The Indians desire peace and they now pledge their honor to maintain it.

If bad men among the whites or among other people, subject to the authority of the United States, will commit any wrong upon the person or property of the Indians, the United States will, upon proof made to the Agent and forwarded to the Commissioner of Indian Affairs at Washington City, proceed at once to cause the offender to be arrested and punished according to the laws of the United States and also reimburse the injured person for the loss sustained.

If bad men among the Indians shall commit a wrong or depredation upon the person or property of any one, white, black or Indian, subject to the authority of the United States and at peace therewith, the Indians herein named, solemnly agree that they

CHAPTER 6

THE LAKOTA LANDING

On March 8, 1964, as a blustery wind churned the waters of San Francisco Bay, a group of American Indians set out on a charter boat for Alcatraz. There, they planned to assert a claim of ownership based on a treaty signed in 1868 between the United States and the Lakota Nation.

But what was this treaty? And why did those Native Americans believe that it mattered?

By definition, a treaty is a legally binding agreement between nations. It has the force of law behind it. In North America, treaties were first made between European colonizers from England and the Native tribal nations of the eastern part of the continent. After the birth of the United States, such treaty making continued between the new nation and the Indigenous peoples who still controlled most of the landmass of the continent. Although written treaties did not exist before the coming of Europeans, Indians often held formal conferences between tribal nations where oral agreements were made. Among some nations, such mnemonic devices as wampum belts made of shell would be created, to symbolize such agreements. However, the large-scale transfer or sale of land from one nation to another was not what those conferences between Indian nations were about.

Obtaining as much Indian land as possible—by cession or by purchase—was the underlying goal of every U.S. Indian treaty. That was true even when the stated purpose of the agreement was the establishment of peace between the formally warring parties, and the treaties were described as being helpful to the Indians.

The number of those agreements formalized between the United States and various Indian tribes is impressive. No fewer than 370 Indian treaties were signed into law between 1778 and 1871.

In April 1869, when Ely S. Parker was appointed by President Ulysses S. Grant to be in charge of American Indian affairs, one of the first actions Parker took was to end the treaty making process. As an Indian himself—a Tonawanda Seneca—he'd observed how all of the power in such agreements rested on the side of the United States. He had seen that the ways these agreements were enforced did not benefit Indians. Parker's hope was that ending these unequal agreements would result in something better for Native Americans. Sadly, that would not happen for many decades.

Parker's unique understanding of the legality of treaties and how they were unfairly interpreted to favor the white side came from his own education. Literate and brilliant, he might have become a lawyer himself, had a law requiring all lawyers in the United States at that time to be citizens not prevented him from doing so. Citizenship would not be granted to all American Indians until decades after his death in 1895.

Contrary to popular culture's depictions of Indians as uneducated, Native Americans were graduating from prestigious colleges as early as the seventeenth century. The first recorded Indian college student was Caleb Cheeshahteaumuck of the Wampanoag Tribe, who graduated from Harvard in 1665. By the late 1960s, the number of Native Americans who had obtained higher education and who were either already lawyers or on their path toward passing the bar was impressive. (Although exact numbers for the 1960s are hard to verify, in 2014 the American Bar Association listed 2,640 Native American attorneys.)

So, when Native Americans began to consider Alcatraz a symbolic and actual site to reclaim as Native land, it was with an educated awareness of treaty law. In particular, there was one treaty that had been signed between the Lakota Nation and the United States that was still in force. That 1868 Treaty of Fort Laramie (based in what is now Wyoming) basically stated that any abandoned federal property could be reclaimed by Native Americans.

Alcatraz, those Indigenous occupiers would argue, was such a place. Although there was still a caretaker on the island, its purpose as a federal prison had been terminated.

Under the specific terms of that 1868 Treaty of Fort Laramie, non-reservation Indians had the right to claim land the government had taken to use for forts and then abandoned. Alcatraz Island fit that description, even though it was far from the Great Plains where that treaty had been signed with the Lakota. The island had, indeed, been a federal fort before it became a federal prison and was now abandoned.

Although it was almost a century after its signing of that treaty, there was no time limit included in that treaty. Further, although the treaty's broad terms had been limited—it did not, for example, apply to Indians in general but only to Lakotas—that was also not a problem.

Like virtually every other major American city where Native Americans had been sent through the government relocation program, the Bay Area was home to a number of Lakota people. It was a group of those Lakotas who, in 1964, decided to take action to test that 1868 treaty.

Led by Belva Cottier, the Lakota group included her husband, Allen Cottier, Garfield Spotted Elk, Walter Means and his son Russell, Richard McKenzie, and Mark Martinez. Joining them were several other non-Lakota Indians from the Bay Area Council—nearly all in "full regalia," the term used by Native Americans to refer to the type of clothing one would wear to traditional ceremonies or to dance at powwows.

Prominent among the non-Lakota was Adam Nordwall, a Native American activist and businessman. Adam had first arrived in San Francisco in 1951. He was a vital and highly visible part of Native life in the Bay Area—he had danced in and emceed powwows, conducted programs for twelve years at San Quentin State Prison for its Indian inmates, taught at a local college, run for Congress, served as a delegate to the Capitol Conference on Poverty in Washington, D.C., and worked with the city's Intertribal Friendship House. In 1962, he had been the major force behind the creation of the United Bay Area Council of American Indians and would serve as its chair for thirteen years.

The Lakota claimants also brought reporters, photographers, and Elliot Leighton. Although non-Native, Leighton already had a reputation as a brilliant activist attorney who was deeply committed to the ideals of Native rights.

When they landed on Alcatraz, they were greeted by A. L. Aylsworth, who was the federal caretaker at the time. When he asked what was going on, he was informed by Leighton that the Lakota were claiming the island based on a federal treaty.

As Adam recalled in his book *Heart of the Rock*, Aylsworth's response was a good-natured: "Well, I guess if you want it, you can have it."

Sioux elder Walter Means staking the occupiers' claim on
Alcatraz and son Russell Means holding the stake, March 9, 1964

Over the next two hours, a number of symbolic activities took place. Allen Cottier read a prepared statement, proclaiming that they were prepared to offer the federal government just compensation for the twenty-two-acre island—at the same rate of forty-seven cents per acre that the federal government was offering California tribes for lands illegally taken from them since the Gold Rush of 1849.

Everyone then went around choosing the sites for their homesteads. Walter Means, with his son Russell, drove in the stakes for his claim. Russell Means, then twenty-six years old, would go on to become one of the most famous American Indians of the later twentieth century. A central figure in the American Indian Movement (AIM), he would be involved in the 1973 Wounded Knee occupation and a movie star in his later years.

On those stakes were hung claims written on pieces of deer hide. Attorney Leighton also had them fill out official claim forms to be sent to the Bureau of Land Management. A tent was set up for the night.

Two things happened soon after. The first was a slow victory dance accompanied by the beating of two drums they'd brought with them. The second, two hours into the occupation, was the arrival of Richard J. Willard, the active warden of Alcatraz.

Willard's demeanor was the opposite of the good-natured Aylsworth. He was infuriated. He informed the Indians and their supporters that they were trespassing and then threatened everyone with arrest if they did not leave immediately. Reinforcements, he told them, would be arriving soon in the form of armed police.

For an hour or two, the Lakota men and women held their ground, sitting in front of their tent. Finally, on Leighton's advice, their occupation ended peacefully. The forty occupiers climbed into their rented boat and headed back to the mainland. On their way, they waved to another vessel heading toward the island. In it were the assistant U.S. attorney and armed U.S. marshals who'd been dispatched to arrest the occupiers. No charges ended up being filed, and although Leighton briefly pursued the claim in court, there was no real follow-up on the part of the Lakotas and it was eventually dismissed.

By the mid-twentieth century, Indians had become increasingly aware of the importance of public opinion.

OF ALL TRIBES

While the federal government seemed deaf to Indian needs, it might start to pay attention if those issues became front-page news and non-Native people began rallying to Indian causes. As the occupiers had hoped, that 1964 event did receive publicity. It briefly drew attention to the legitimate issue of Indian land claims. But it was not taken seriously, and by the next news cycle, it was pretty much forgotten by the general public.

However, it was not forgotten by the Native Americans of the Bay Area. Although that 1964 action had not been intended to result in a permanent occupation, the idea of taking Alcatraz—really taking it next time—was on the minds of many Indians.

CHAPTER 7

THREE ACTIVISTS

Of those Indians involved in the planning and carrying out of the November invasion of Alcatraz, three figures stand out. Their names are Adam Nordwall (later Adam Fortunate Eagle), Richard Oakes, and LaNada Means (later LaNada War Jack). To fully understand the roles they played, both at Alcatraz and in later years, it's helpful to know their backgrounds: where they came from and what forces shaped them into who they became.

Adam Nordwall: The Planner and Publicist
"I was always thinking of Alcatraz."
Adam Fortunate Eagle, 2022

OF ALL TRIBES

The Red Lake Indian Reservation in northwestern Minnesota belongs to the Red Lake Band of Chippewa Indians—Ojibwe, as they prefer to be called. Red Lake's twelve hundred square miles is home to about six thousand band members, with an equal number living off reservation. It's the home community of Adam Nordwall, an enrolled Ojibwe and the son of a Swedish father and an Ojibwe woman. By 1969, he had become what the U.S. government might call an Indian success story.

When he was five, Adam's father died, and his mother had no choice but to send him and his four siblings to a government school—the Pipestone Indian Training School in Pipestone, Minnesota. He arrived there in 1935. As he explained in his 2010 autobiography, *Pipestone, My Life in an Indian Boarding School*, it could not have been a better time to be at that school. In 1934, John Collier, the idealistic Commissioner of Indian Affairs, had instituted sweeping changes in the federal Indian boarding school system. "No interference with Indian religious life or expression will be tolerated," Collier stated. Because Pipestone had federal funding, as Adam explained in his book *Heart of the Rock*, "we were not forced as other kids in missionary schools had been, to see our families as 'sinful pagans.'"

Nordwall's good fortune continued when he went on to Haskell Institute in Lawrence, Kansas. By then, Haskell had become a school that provided useful education at a higher level, a combination of high school and junior college, for its Native students. It would eventually go on to become Haskell Indian Nations University.

At Haskell, Nordwall took courses in commercial art and met a young Shoshone woman from the Fallon Reservation in Nevada, Bobbi Graham, who was studying secretarial arts. As was often the case in boarding schools when Native young people from different nations were brought together, he and Bobbi fell in love and married in 1948. Adam got his first job that winter drawing magazine advertisements for Centaur Studios in Kansas City.

In 1951, Adam's mother, who had moved to San Francisco, asked them to join her. Adam's four older brothers had been called up to serve in the Korean War. His mother assumed Adam would soon be drafted. Before that happened, she wanted him and his wife, now expecting their first child, to spend time with her. She had found a temporary job with an exterminating company that Adam could try out. Though they waited, that call to the military never came, and Adam did so well that his job became permanent. By the late 1960s, he was president and general manager of his own East Bay termite exterminating firm, employing fifteen people and driving a Cadillac.

Business, though, was far from Adam's first interest. His aim had never been to give up his Native identity and blend into the white world. As more and more young reservation Indians arrived in the Bay Area through the federal relocation program, Adam became involved in the growing Native community. He went to powwows, made contacts with other local Indians, observed traditional dancing, and began to take part wearing his own makeshift regalia. His regalia and his knowledge grew more and more authentic as other local older Ojibwes, such as Cy and Aggie Williams, took an interest in this outgoing young man and began to teach him traditional ways. Cy and Aggie were from the Cass Lake Reservations, fifty miles southeast of Adam's Red Lake community. The contacts he made helped him develop the United Bay Area Council, which unified the numerous Native American groups already existing in the Bay Area into "an Indian mini-version of the United Nations." The classes he taught on Native history at local colleges widened his contacts even further, as did his volunteer work at San Quentin State Prison, where the Indian inmates club he worked with had originally been sponsored by one of the guards, a burly Native Hawaiian man named E. E. Papke who became a close friend.

Another friend Adam made during those years was a young Vietnam veteran working as a Volunteers in Service to America (VISTA) volunteer, Tim Findley. VISTA was founded in 1965, as part of President Lyndon Johnson's "war on poverty" legislation, a set of government programs designed to help poor Americans. Now known as AmericorpsVISTA and operating in all fifty states, its volunteers help local organizations fight poverty.

Tim had also participated in the civil rights movement as a freedom rider and was committed to equal rights for all Americans, including Indians. Adam had met Tim while the young idealist was working on a project for the federal Office of Economic Opportunity (OEO), a film about conditions on American Indian reservations. Findley planned to screen it before the United Council. However, the decision was made by the OEO that the film was too accurate in its depiction of the terrible conditions on those reservations. Against Findley's angry objections, the film was withdrawn and never shown. The one good thing that came out of it was a lasting friendship between Adam and Tim, one that would prove helpful for the Indians of All Tribes.

Being an accomplished and highly visible powwow dancer and emcee suited Adam well. At heart, he was a showman. He loved being in the public eye, especially when he could use it as an opportunity to draw attention to Native concerns. The cover of *Alcatraz, Alcatraz*, the first book he would write about the 1969 takeover of the prison island, features a photograph of him in full dance regalia.

Although being in the public eye appealed to Adam, he didn't believe in violent confrontation. Rather than the militant, weapon-carrying stance of the Black Panthers, founded in 1966 in Oakland, Adam chose to make his point while making people laugh. As he explained to me in a March 2022 interview, "Our tactic was to use satire and humor as a weapon."

His first public use of that approach occurred the year before the Indians of All Tribes took over Alcatraz Island. The annual San Francisco Columbus Day celebration was a big event in the city. Joe Cevetto, a good-natured Italian

American, played the part of Columbus each year. His outfit as the Genoese navigator even included a wig to cover his balding head. Each year, he would step ashore to claim America by ritually thrusting a staff into the sandy beach. By 1967, Nordwall's Native dance group was also part of the celebration. In 1968, Adam staged an unexpected ending to the event. As soon as "Columbus" had planted his staff, he stepped in. "Bend down a second, Joe," he whispered. Then, as Cevetto dropped to all fours, Adam reached out, yanked off his wig, and brandished it over his head—scalping Columbus. People roared with laughter, and cameras flashed as the event's emcee read a prepared statement, written by Adam, about the disastrous effects of colonialism on American Indians.

Richard Oakes: The Public Face
"Alcatraz is not an island. It's an idea."
Richard Oakes, 1969

OF ALL TRIBES

The Akwesasne Mohawk Reservation was the birthplace of Richard Oakes. Squeezed between Canada and the United States, Akwesasne is located at the extreme northern tip of what is now New York State. Only four miles long, part of the reservation lies in Canada and part in the United States.

On the U.S. side, it's officially known as the St. Regis Mohawk Reservation. On the Canadian side, it is the St.

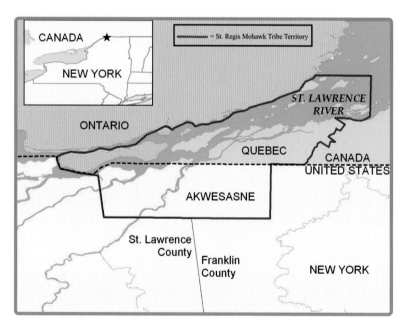

A map of Akwesasne St. Regis Mohawk Tribe Territory, which lies in both Canada and the U.S.

Regis Mohawk Reserve No. 9. Of its approximately twelve thousand tribal members, about three thousand are in the United States and nine thousand in Canada. On the reservation's Cornwall Island, in the St. Lawrence River, a person can stand with one foot in one country and one foot in the other. Although their traditional name for themselves is Kanien'keha:ka, People of the Flint, Mohawk is the name most commonly used by the public and by the Mohawks themselves. Called Saint Regis by white governments, their divided reservation is known as Akwesasne, the Place Where the Partridge Drums, to its Indigenous people.

In the Great League of the Haudenosaunee, originally composed of five Iroquois-speaking tribes—the Seneca, Cayuga, Oneida, Onondaga, and Mohawk (later a sixth tribe, the Tuscarora, was added)—the Mohawk are known as the Keepers of the Eastern Door, reflecting their place as the easternmost of the original nations in an alliance symbolized by the shape of a longhouse. Until the American Revolution, the league was a major force, politically and militarily, in the Northeast.

Akwesasne is not the traditional homeland of its Native residents. After the American Revolution, during which many Mohawks took the side of the British, their tribal nation was forced out of their communities in the Mohawk Valley of New York State, ending up at Akwesasne, nearby Kahnawake, and other Canadian reserves.

The main bridge that goes from Canada to the United States is on St. Regis Mohawk Reservation land. According to the Jay Treaty of 1794 between Canada and the young United States, it was agreed that the Iroquois would be able to pass back and forth between the United States and Canada without hindrance. Because that agreement is not always honored, symbolic border crossings have been staged for many decades by Iroquois people on that bridge.

Iroquois activism and the defense of their rights were modeled for the young Richard Oakes by such people as Levi General/Deskaheh, a hereditary Cayuga chief and appointed speaker. Deskaheh traveled to Geneva, Switzerland, in 1923, where he addressed the League of Nations in an attempt to secure justice for his Haudenosaunee people.

In 1969, a group called the White Roots of Peace was created. Its name was drawn from the image of the great pine tree symbolically planted when the five original warring nations of the Iroquois, Mohawk, Oneida, Onondaga, Cayuga, and

Seneca joined together in peace more than one thousand years ago. The White Roots of Peace traveled throughout the United States, speaking for Indigenous rights and against pollution and environmental destruction. Tom Porter from Akwesasne, Mad Bear Anderson from the Tuscarora, Alice Papineau/Dewasentah from Onondaga, and Peter Mitten from Cayuga were among the spiritual teachers on that journey, as well as Jerry Gambill/Rarihokwats, the founder of the activist Native newspaper *Akwesasne Notes*. The trip included a September visit to California, where they stayed with Richard Oakes and his family.

There was also another way in which Mohawk men regularly found themselves in contact with American majority culture—ironwork. In 1886, the Victoria Bridge for the Canadian Pacific Railroad was being constructed across the St. Lawrence River by the Kahnawake Reservation. So many Mohawk men walked out on that bridge while it was under construction, asking the workers how they were doing, that some were given jobs. Ironwork came to Mohawks almost naturally. Working at great heights didn't seem to bother them. It wasn't that they lacked fear; they just never let it stop them. The fact that it was dangerous made it more attractive to men coming from a long tradition of risking their lives to protect their people in war.

The reputation of Mohawks in high steel spread, and so did the demand for them in a nation where taller and taller skyscrapers were being built. A branch of the steel workers union, Iron Workers Local 40, was created and still exists on the Kahnawake Reservation. Skywalking, as they described it, became the dominant trade followed by young Mohawk men. For more than a century, all across the continent, Mohawks have been involved in the construction of skyscrapers, from the first tall buildings in New York City to the present day.

By 1960, an estimated eight hundred Mohawk ironworkers and their families were living in Brooklyn in the Boerum Hill area, known locally as Little Kahnawake. A branch of the Iron Workers Union Brooklyn Local 361 was made up primarily of Mohawks.

Richard Oakes's ironworker father had left his family and moved to Brooklyn. Richard's mother, Irene, was forced to place Richard and his brother Leonard in a Syracuse orphanage until she could locate work and a suitable home for them.

THREE ACTIVISTS

Richard's life as a child was divided between time in Brooklyn and at Akwesasne. At the age of sixteen, he entered the iron-working trade himself as a catcher, someone who would catch the white-hot rivets thrown to him and then pass them on to the men who would jackhammer them into the steel girders. Even more than his peers, he liked courting danger. The St. Lawrence River is wide and has treacherous currents at Akwesasne, but that did not prevent the teenage Richard from swimming across it and back.

Oakes was also deeply affected by the words of his elders. They created in him a lasting awareness of the long tradition of Iroquois being leaders and defenders of their people. By the time he was in his twenties, he looked the part of a modern-day Hiawatha. Tall, dark-haired, handsome, and muscular, he stood out in any crowd.

He also never backed down from a brawl and usually was the one who came out on top. As a child and then an adult, he was often targeted by law enforcement because he was Mohawk. In those days on both the Canadian and the U.S. side, equal justice was seldom applied to Indians by the Horsemen (the Royal Mounted Police) or the New York State Troopers. In the boarding and residential schools of both nations, there was terrible abuse when it came to Native kids. In the 1950s and 1960s, neither national system was on the side of Indigenous people.

In 1959, just before his eighteenth birthday, Richard and two other Mohawk boys stole a meat truck in Syracuse and drove it to the Onondaga Reservation. After getting there, the other boys ran off, but Richard stayed, handing out free steaks and hamburger meat until the police came and arrested him. Fortunately for him, when he came to trial, the judge showed rare understanding. Because of his age and the generosity of his actions, he was given a short sentence to be served at the Elmira Reformatory.

After his release, Richard began hanging out with a tough crowd of young Indians in Brooklyn. In 1962, he was targeted by a policeman with a reputation for beating Indians. Richard fought back until police backup arrived and he was arrested. Falsely charged with assault and robbery, he was sentenced to three years at the maximum-security Great Meadow Correctional Facility in Comstock, New York. His reputation as a tough guy served him well in prison, as other inmates quickly learned it was not a good idea to mess with Oakes. Within that first year of his sentence, the trumped-up charge of robbery was dropped. He was released and went back to ironworking.

Well-paying and prestigious as his job in construction was, Richard was not satisfied. He'd gained a legendary reputation at his home reservation of Akwesasne as a charismatic charmer, handsome and gentlemanly as well as unwilling to back down from a fight or tolerate injustice. But he wanted to do more with his life, to truly make a difference.

Finding ways to stand up for Indians, Richard decided, was the way to do it. In 1967, the Lakota writer and activist Vine Deloria, Jr., executive director of the National Congress of American Indians, sanctioned the use of the term "Red Power," an idea that galvanized Richard. Realizing he needed more education to be informed and effective, he began taking community college classes and night classes at Syracuse University.

Finally, in 1968, wanting

Richard Oakes being interviewed by a local news station

to see more of the country and understand more of what other Indians were experiencing, he quit his job, sold his ironworking tools, and purchased a 1965 red Ford Mustang. Packing up his few belongings, he headed west. As he crossed the country, he stopped at one reservation after another, seeing for himself how many things all American Indians had in common—not just a history of oppression but also the need for an appreciation of their own cultures and traditional values. He arrived in San Francisco in time to experience the mammoth student protests on the San Francisco State College campus after the firing of a Black faculty member. In 1969, he became one of the first Indians to enroll in the college's new Native American studies program. He immediately proved to be a charismatic student leader with a flair for public speaking.

Unlike Adam, with his love of striking regalia, Richard dressed simply. One of the few times he wore anything more than street clothes was at the pier in San Francisco before the Indians of All Tribes made their first attempt to take Alcatraz. Just as Richard was about to deliver their proclamation, Adam handed him a beaded headband "to add some dash to his handsomely thick dark hair" before he began to speak.

THREE ACTIVISTS

LaNada Means (War Jack) : The Rebel
"I was a student and a mother and I had a lot of things to do and it was really good to have Richard there and have him do the work that he was doing and he did a really awesome job."
LaNada Means (War Jack) , January 20, 2022

LaNada Means earned an early reputation as a rebel. It could be said that it was in her blood. Her people, the Bannocks, had resisted the loss of their lands and their freedom in the eighteenth century. Like many of the other tribes of the Northwest, the Oregon Trail passed through their traditional homelands. Their hunting and food gathering areas, as LaNada explained it, "were pillaged by both cavalry and immigrants." Despite their attempts to live in peace with white people, one war after another was fought against them. The Bannocks did not give up easily. They gained the reputation of being the most determined warriors among the northwest Shoshone nations. One of their greatest war chiefs was Tanmonmah, also known as War Jack. As a young

LaNada Means (War Jack) with her son Deynon on the *Seaweed*. Richard Oakes is at left.

warrior, he took part in the Pyramid Lake War of 1860 and the Modoc War of 1872–1873. He then allied with the Sioux and the Cheyenne in the Battle of the Little Bighorn in 1877. He went on to play a major role in the Bannock War of 1878 and the so-called Sheepeater Indian War of 1879 as his people struggled to hold on to their lands.

After his surrender, War Jack agreed to a treaty that he was told would give his people title to what had been much of their traditional lands. Then he was put in jail. Ironically, considering LaNada's later involvement with the prison island, the government's plan was to exile War Jack to Alcatraz as a prisoner of war. It was only the intercession of the army generals who had been his adversaries and admired him for his honor and courage that caused him to be released before being sent to prison.

That promise to return tribal lands, however, was never kept. Instead, the Fort Hall Indian Reservation, which had originally covered 1.8 million acres, was reduced in size as railway cessions took thousands of acres and white squatters were given title to parts of the reservation land by the state of Idaho. Today, only five hundred thousand acres of the reservation remain, though parts of it are still constantly being leased and taken from the tribe by the Bureau of Indian Affairs. Of the approximately six thousand people living on the reservation, almost two thousand identify as non-Indian.

LaNada Boyer, as she was known for her first eighteen years, was born in 1947 on that Fort Hall Shoshone Bannock Reservation in Idaho. She was part of the first generation of her people to be raised speaking the foreign tongue of English. Her father, who was deeply aware of the Bannock history of resistance, had been a tribal chairman. Although it turned the Bureau of Indian Affairs against him and eventually cost him his office, he fought against the continuing government policies that hurt his people, such as the practice of tribal termination. (Before the Alcatraz takeover, there had been a long list of tribes targeted for the next round of termination. That list included both Adam's Red Lake Chippewa and LaNada's Fort Hall Shoshone Bannock.)

So it was that LaNada grew up knowing she came from a background of rebellion, inspired by War Jack and her own father. Her rebellion was not so much against the United States and its schools as it was in favor of her own identity and her Indian people.

While LaNada was always an outstanding student, on the honor roll of every institution she attended, she was also a rebel. This was a time when stores throughout the Northwest routinely displayed signs that read NO INDIANS OR DOGS ALLOWED. But she always remembered her father's words to her: "Before you start school, I want you to know that you are an Indian. Don't ever be ashamed of who you are, because this whole country belongs to us."

By the time she was seventeen, she had been expelled

from school after school. Looking back years later, she saw that her pain at the way she, her brothers and sisters, and other Native kids were treated "turned into rebellion." Sent at thirteen to St. Mary's Episcopal School in South Dakota, she was on the honor roll but expelled for having a pack of cigarettes. After starting high school in Blackfoot, Idaho, she was expelled for violating curfew after just a few months, despite getting good grades. It was there that she started stealing cars with her Indian friends. They would hot-wire the cars, drive them to the reservations, and then play their own form of demolition derby before pushing the stolen vehicles off cliffs into the river. This got her arrested on several occasions. But she had learned what to say and when to say it by then, and she managed each time to talk her way out of conviction with a sympathetic judge while her Indian friends ended up being sent to reform school.

Despite her rebellious behavior, she knew she had to find a way to get through school. So, at the age of sixteen, she enrolled in Chilocco Indian School in Oklahoma. Once again, within six weeks, she was on the honor roll. The captain of the football team and senior class president became her boyfriend, a romance that continued even after the boys' dean told her boyfriend to stop seeing her because she was the wrong kind of girl. She began to build up demerits for such things as imperfect room inspections. She was banned from any function aside from attending classes and was reassigned to the "bad girls" dorm, thirteen students who, like her, were not from Oklahoma and became her best friends. Eventually, once again, she was expelled. When her father met her at the bus station, she apologized for getting kicked out of school yet again. His response was that it was okay. She'd resisted being programmed and brainwashed, and he was glad to welcome her home.

Her unsuccessful journey through high school was not quite over. She enrolled in Blackfoot High School one more time—and was expelled yet again. Offered the chance to attend Haskell Indian School, the same school where Adam Nordwall gained his degree in commercial art, she turned it down. After being kicked out of school half a dozen times, "I already knew the story and just wanted to skip it this time."

She then began seeking work in the nearby town of Blackfoot. But she was turned down every time she saw a sign in a restaurant window reading WAITRESS NEEDED. Then she got an idea. She went to a white friend who worked in a beauty shop and had her black hair dyed blonde. Going back to the last restaurant that had turned her down, this time as a blonde with a tan and not an Indian, she was immediately hired.

Passing for white, though, was not how she wanted to live her life. Having heard she could take a test and get a high school diploma, she paid the ten-dollar test fee, took the test at Idaho State College, and was awarded a high school diploma in 1963. Thinking she was finally on her way, at the age of seventeen, she enrolled in the nearest college to her reservation. After one semester, though, not having learned the necessary academic discipline from her past difficult high school experiences and finding it hard to get transportation to and from school, she decided to "try again another time."

Finally, in January 1965, she returned home, got on the BIA relocation program, and went to San Francisco, thinking this would provide the opportunity she needed. She quickly learned that for all the government's promises, the relocation plan was meant not to advance Indians but to "assimilate us and disenfranchise us from our reservation lands and our membership with our tribes." However, being part of the growing Indian community in the Bay Area taught her how much all Native Americans had in common. She learned, as she put it in her autobiography, "You all are Native and that is all that counts." She began visiting the San Francisco American Indian Center and its events, hearing of and experiencing intertribal powwows for the first time. She also became involved with the Indian Historical Society, after finding it listed in the phone book. She worked with its founders, Rupert Costo (Cahuilla) and Jeanette Costo (Cherokee), first going to meetings and speaking in schools and then writing articles. Her advocacy work grew, though she sometimes found herself at odds with other Natives who had bought into European American ideas of male chauvinism and resented her speaking up.

By 1967, despite her advocacy work, she had little money and was living in San Francisco as a single mother on a program called Aid to Families with Dependent Children (AFDC). She was now using the last name of Means, though she was estranged from her sons' father—a brother of the same Russell Means who had taken part in the 1964 Lakota claim on Alcatraz Island. Her older son, Devon, born in 1965, was with her parents in Idaho. Her second child, Deynon, born in 1967, was with her. She'd tried, without success, to enroll first at San Francisco State and then the City College of San Francisco. Then she heard that some of the Black youths she knew were being given the chance through the Educational Opportunity Program to enroll in the University of California at Berkeley. She applied with the support of a local minister and was given conditional acceptance. In January 1968, LaNada Means became the first American Indian student at UCB. And this time, her educational experience would be far different.

That first quarter, she maintained a 3.0 average and helped recruit more Indian students. She organized a Native American Students Organization and was elected as its chair. Then came the strike.

A coalition of Black, Chicano, Asian, and Native American students had joined together to ask for the creation of ethnic studies departments and more diversity overall at the university. The student body majority joined in support of their cause to the university, which refused to hear their request. It resulted in the campus-wide Third World Liberation Front strike in January 1969, as well as similar student strikes and picketing at other California campuses for the same goals.

UC Berkeley refused at first to listen to the coalition's demands. It responded by using the campus police to try to break up the picketing. Then, when that did not work, the university brought in the National Guard, which marched onto campus with bayonets unsheathed. All classes and activities on the campus were shut down and the Berkeley leaders of the Third World Liberation Front, including LaNada, were arrested and briefly detained. The strike, however, went on. Finally, after forty-nine days, the UCB president agreed to discuss their demands. Then, as a member of the four-person negotiation team, LaNada helped forge the agreement that created four new programs, in Black, Chicano, Asian, and Native American studies, the first such programs in the UC system.

Although she was suspended for six months, LaNada was not expelled. By September 1969, she was back at Berkeley as a full-time student.

Her role in the student protests and in creating the first-ever American Indian Studies Program, combined with her experiences working with the Indian Historian Press, all prepared her to be among those who proposed and carried out the taking of Alcatraz. In many ways, perhaps more than any other person, she would be the heart of the Indians of All Tribes. In the often-changing group of occupiers, she would be the only one who remained throughout the entire nineteen months.

Occupiers unloading the boat onto the water barge at Alcatraz

CHAPTER 8

TAKING THE ROCK

In the American popular imagination, California is a mythical place. It's been called the Golden State, not just for the precious mineral that drew so many thousands of people in search of wealth. Its warm climate and its reputation as a place of unlimited opportunity have drawn people of all classes and races to go there in search of a better life.

San Francisco, the city by the bay, has held a special place in that image of California as the Promised Land. Celebrated in story and song, there's no doubting its beauty. But the real San Francisco is a much more complicated place. Racial and social inequity have always been part of its reality. In 1969, nowhere was that more obvious than in the part of the city known as the Mission District. There, in substandard housing occupied by the poorest of the poor—many of them belonging to so-called minority populations—lived most of San Francisco's Indian population.

The 1960s in the United States were a chaotic and often violent period in which the struggle for equal rights for African Americans was at its peak. Between 1963 and 1968, the decade saw the assassinations of President John F. Kennedy, Martin Luther King, Jr., Malcolm X, and the president's brother Senator Robert Kennedy. The Vietnam War seemed to be never-ending in Southeast Asia, and thousands of American soldiers were dying. In response to those calls for equal rights and an end to the Vietnam War, marches and mass student protests—often met with violence by the authorities—took place on university and college campuses. Prior to the Alcatraz takeover, one of the largest of those student protests occurred at San Francisco State College in 1967, after the firing of George Murray, an instructor at the college. Murray was a member of the Black Panthers, a political organization that challenged police brutality against African Americans and engaged in social programs intended to improve the lives of urban Black people.

It was also a time when American Indians were being romanticized in popular culture, seen as somehow better and purer than "civilized" white people. That stereotype ignored the fact that Native Americans have always been people—human beings with their own weaknesses and strengths, dreams, and desires. San Francisco's Haight-Ashbury district was full of hippies—young men and women who believed in all kinds of freedoms, dressed in elaborate clothes, sometimes even pretending to be Indians. The idea of anarchy was in the air, the belief that the best of all worlds was one in which there were no authorities and you could do whatever you wanted.

It was in that complicated atmosphere of the late 1960s that many, Indian and non-Native alike, were drawn to Alcatraz. There are many myths about Alcatraz. One is that its waters are un-swimmable and shark-infested. In fact, there are no sharks around the island. It is, simply, biologically impossible. There are indeed very large great white sharks in the Farallon Islands thirty miles beyond the Golden Gate Bridge, but the waters of the San Francisco Bay are so mixed with freshwater that it is not possible for sharks to survive there.

Although there are riptides off the beaches of San

Francisco that make swimming there hazardous and the tides do come in and out of the bay with considerable force, it is more than possible to swim the two miles from Alcatraz to the mainland or vice versa. It's a feat that takes anywhere from twenty minutes to an hour for a well-prepared swimmer—wearing a wetsuit. Since the bay's waters vary seasonally from 45 to 65 degrees, hypothermia would be the result of attempting that swim without thermal insulation.

In fact, every year "Sharkfest" races are held for competitors to swim around the rock. Innumerable people have made that swim from the mainland to the prison island or in the opposite direction—with the help of a knowledge of the tides and dangerous currents. And not just adults have done that. The youngest person (carefully monitored by adults) to swim to Alcatraz was a nine-year-old named James Savage.

In 1964, Alcatraz had been declared surplus property by the federal government to be given to the city of San Francisco. The Bay Area United Council of Indians came up with a proposal for Adam Norwall to present to the federal government. The five-point plan for the island included "a vocational training center, an Indian museum, and a spiritual facility."

Two things happened then that changed everything. The

first, in September 1969, was a proposal by the Texas billionaire Lamar Hunt. His plan was to purchase Alcatraz and turn the island into a huge tourist attraction. There would be high-priced apartments, a restaurant, and a space-age museum. The San Francisco Board of Supervisors liked that plan and quickly voted to approve it.

The second thing that occurred was a fire. In October 1969, the San Francisco American Indian Center, the most important meeting place for Bay Area Indians, burned to the ground. No one knows what caused it, though some speculated it was arson.

The United Bay Area Council met soon after in a temporary location, an old glass-walled storefront. With Adam as one of the prominent voices at the meeting, the council came to a decision. At virtually the same time, a similar plan was put together by the group of Native students spearheaded by LaNada and Richard. Together, it was decided that these young people would be the ones who carried out the plan in the name of the Indians of All Tribes. They would occupy the former prison island, claiming it as Indian land.

The trip on the morning of November 9 was designed as a spectacle, a reflection of Adam's showmanship. But that

OF ALL TRIBES

morning of November 9, Adam, wearing his flower-beaded yoke and porcupine quill roach headpiece, was getting very nervous. As many as seventy Indians had gathered, including dancers in regalia and a drummer. A motorized launch with reporters and cameramen was cruising back and forth waiting for the Indians to set out for Alcatraz. But there was a big problem. The boats that Adam had arranged to take them to the island had not shown up.

Adam saw that the press needed something to focus on. He handed Richard Oakes two things. The first was a red headband to make him look more striking. The second was the proclamation that had been prepared for the occasion. Climbing up onto a pier post, Richard began to read:

> We, the Native Americans, reclaim the land known as Alcatraz Island in the name of all American Indians by right of discovery. We wish to be fair and honorable in our dealings with the Caucasian inhabitants of this land, and hereby offer the following treaty:
>
> We will purchase said Alcatraz Island for $24 in glass beads and red cloth, a precedent set by the white man's purchase of a similar island about 300

years ago. We know that $24 in trade goods for these 16 acres is more than what was paid when Manhattan Island was sold, but we know that land values have risen over the years. Our offer of $1.24 per acre is greater than the $.47 per acre the white men are now paying the California Indians for their land. We will give to the inhabitants of this land a portion of that land for their own, to be held in trust by the American Indian government—for as long as the sun shall rise and the rivers go down to the sea—to be administered by the Bureau of Caucasian affairs BCA. We will further guide the inhabitants in the proper way of living. We will offer them our religion, our education, our life ways, in order to help them achieve our level of civilization and thus raise them and all their white brothers up from their savage and unhappy state. We offer this treaty in good faith and wish to be fair and honorable in our dealings with all white men.

While Richard read, Nordwall was running up and down the docks trying to find a boat that would take them to Alcatraz.

Then, Adam saw it. A beautiful little schooner named *Monte Christo*, after the romantic Alexander Dumas novel, *The Count of Monte Christo*. It even had a cannon. And its white Canadian skipper, Ronald Craig, was as dramatically clad, dressed to the nines in eighteenth-century nautical style—with a white billowy shirt, a lacy tie, a hugely oversized belt, and a sword hanging on his side. He truly did look like Dumas' romantic Count.

After a brief negotiation, during which Adam explained they simply wanted to take a little sail out close to Alcatraz (with no mention of any plans to take it over) Captain Craig agreed but said he could take no more than fifty passengers. As the captain and Adam counted them, that was just about how many Indians piled on board.

Soon, the party of would-be invaders was underway, the cannon fired to herald their departure. Trailed by the motor launch and several other boats packed with the media, they soon neared Alcatraz's rocky shores.

All had gone well until then. But bringing the boat to the dock had not been in the agreement with Captain Craig. After a second pass, a hundred yards from Alcatraz, he began turning back toward the city. That was when, perhaps suspecting something, Craig asked Adam in a rather worried voice, "Say, nobody's going to jump off or anything."

"Oh no," Nordwall replied.

But he was wrong, for that was when the scenario changed. Without even taking off his boots, Richard Oakes dove into the water and began to swim toward the island, followed by four other men.

It's at this juncture that the history of what happened differs slightly. Adam would write, three decades later, that Richard never made it to Alcatraz on that first attempt and was pulled choking and sputtering out of the water back onto the media launch. It was only when they were closer to the island that Richard jumped back in and struggled to shore on his second attempt.

Richard himself, and other Indians who were there, described what happened differently. They say that he made it to the island on his first try—along with three of the four others, Joe Bill, Ross Harden, and Jim Bob. The fourth man, Walter Heads, could not make it and was pulled back on board the ship. Oakes described it as the toughest swim he ever made.

Meanwhile, *Monte Cristo*, along with Adam and the

other forty-five Indians, was well on its way back to the San Francisco pier.

At that time, the only person on Alcatraz was the current caretaker, John Hart, who had once been the assistant warden and regularly patrolled the shoreline with his large dog. Oakes and his three companions were all discovered by Hart and told "to get the hell off the island." They were soon taken back to the mainland by another boat. Despite the fact that they had been caught trespassing, they were released without any charges being filed. But that was not the end of the story for that day.

Although the Coast Guard and the press thought it was over, more was to happen that same day of November 9. Another boat was found. It was the *New Vera II*, a long-railed fishing boat usually used for salmon charters. Its skipper, Jerry Best, was someone Adam had known for a long time. Adam and his two brothers had been hired by him in the past to do salmon fishing. The skipper agreed to take the group to Alcatraz at $3.50 a head for the round trip. The fee was then paid. Half was put up by Adam and half by Earl Livermore, the Blackfeet director of the San Francisco American Indian Center.

Twenty-five Indians boarded that boat at Fisherman's Wharf that evening, including a late-arriving Richard, who had gone home for a change of clothes, a sleeping bag, and some food. With him was a small group of San Francisco State Native students.

The trip across the cold darkening waters on that day was a chilly one, but they were soon at the Alcatraz dock. As the captain tied up his ship, Richard, LaNada, and twelve others quickly made their way onto the dock. When the captain realized what was happening, he panicked. Perhaps he was afraid his boat would be confiscated by the Coast Guard or that he would be charged with criminal trespass. For whatever reason, he reversed his engines and pulled away from the dock, breaking the rope and leaving eleven of the would-be occupiers, including Earl Livermore and Adam Nordwall, still on the boat.

Of those first fourteen young occupiers, five were from San Francisco State, six from Berkeley, and three from the San Francisco American Indian Center. The Native nations they represented—Cherokee, Shoshone/Bannock, Pueblo, Lakota, Winnebago, Creek, Sac and Fox, Colville, and Mohawk—were a cross section of American

Indian culture. Richard Oakes described what happened next:

> We landed at about 6 o'clock and hid. I guess the caretaker was alerted that we had landed. He, his three patrolmen, and their ferocious guard dog came out and tried to find us. There were 14 of us hiding in the grass and [at] times they passed within inches of us. Even with their dog they couldn't detect us. We could see the dog, wagging his tail and barking occasionally. I guess he was used to us by then.
>
> They soon gave up the search, and we split into three groups just to be safe. Some of us slept outside and some in the buildings. It was cold that night. The next morning we did a lot of exploring, looking for food, wood supplies, places to sleep, and generally getting the lay of the land for the next landing. The place was desolate. It was so rundown it was already beginning to feel like a reservation.

Meanwhile, back at the wharf, Adam had called his reporter friend Tim Findley to tell him about the occupation.

Findley put in a call to John Hart, the Alcatraz caretaker, and asked him about the Indians on the island.

Hart's immediate reply was, "What Indians? There aren't any more Indians."

Knowing that authorities would soon arrive, Richard, LaNada, and the twelve other Indian students agreed to split up and hide. There were plenty of places for that. As LaNada observed: "On the island, you can hide just about anywhere, and no one can find you. And they would be coming by so close, and it was almost like someone would be tickling you and you would be trying to keep back your laughter because you didn't want to give yourself away. We felt like such kids."

They hid so well that no Indians could be seen when a large group of people arrived on the island, including not just the press corps but the Coast Guard and T. E. Hannon, the regional director for the General Services Administration (GSA), the agency in charge of the island.

As LaNada explained, "We could see them, the press and all those feds, and they were looking for us, but we were still hiding out, and nobody could be found."

In fact, rather than finding the Indians, the Indians found them. As Tim Findley leaned back against a wall in the main cellblock to light a cigarette, a voice spoke up from behind him.

"Hey, Tim."

Startled, the reporter turned around to see Richard Oakes sticking his head out of the window.

"Who are those guys," Oakes asked.

"Feds," Findley replied. "And some guy from GSA who wants to talk to you."

Findley then informed Richard that the Coast Guard was ready to arrest the occupiers unless they agreed to leave peacefully.

It was at that point that Oakes made a difficult decision. He agreed to give up and help find the other Indians. It seemed like a betrayal to some. As LaNada expressed it, "Richard gave us up. The press arrived, and Richard gets up and declares himself the leader and gives us all up. When we got back I had to explain to the other students, who were ready to come over the next day, what happened."

Others saw his point. An occupation could not be sustained with only fourteen people and no supplies. Richard understood that the movement might die if they were all arrested. Their mission had achieved its main purpose—

to gather intelligence on what infrastructure remained on the island and what would be needed for a long-term take-over.

———

It would be better to return prepared on another day.

The fourteen occupiers, accompanied by the press, made their way to the docks, where the Coast Guard and Hannon were waiting.

Seeing the opportunity to use the moment like a press conference, Richard pulled out the proclamation. Striking a dramatic pose, Oakes read it again—from its beginning to its ironically accurate final words:

We feel this so-called Alcatraz Island is more than suitable as an Indian reservation, as determined by the white man's own standards. By this we mean this place resembles most Indian reservations, in that:

1. It is isolated from modern facilities, and without adequate means of transportation.

2. It has no fresh running water.

3. It has inadequate sanitation facilities.

4. There are no oil or mineral rights.

5. There is no industry and so unemployment is very great.

6. There are no healthcare facilities.

7. The soil is rocky and non-productive and the land does not support game.

8. There are no educational facilities.

9. The population has always exceeded the land base.

10. The population has always been held as prisoners and kept dependent upon others.

Further, it would be fitting and symbolic that ships of all over the world, entering the Golden Gate, would see Indian land, and thus be reminded of the true history of this nation. This tiny island would be a symbol of the great lands once ruled by free and noble Indians.

That observation of Alcatraz being as poor as a reservation was an accurate one. Most Indian reservations back then were desperately poor and lacking in all those things listed on the proclamation. The prison island was also in terrible shape. It was far different from what it had been in the early 1960s. The total lack of upkeep had resulted in the kind of deterioration one might expect from negligent maintenance. In the damp salty air of the bay, wood had rotted and metal and steel had eroded. In many places, rusted reinforcing bars were exposed. Blackberry vines grew around the railings, and the catwalks along the cellblock seemed ready to fall off. When government negotiators later told the Indian occupiers of the prison island that it was not a safe place, they were not exaggerating.

After reading the proclamation, the fourteen occupiers climbed onto the Coast Guard vessel and were taken back to San Francisco, where no charges were filed and they were allowed to leave. The authorities thought it was over. But they were wrong.

The publicity the occupiers had received was generally positive. The news coverage of their second attempt of the day to reclaim the prison island had been even greater than their first try. The reactions by the authorities to both of their attempts had been mild.

OF ALL TRIBES

After that second November 9 trip to Alcatraz, the student activists were feeling energized. And their attempts had galvanized the Bay Area Indian community.

———

Dean Chavers, a Lumbee Indian veteran of two tours in Vietnam and a student in Berkeley's new Native American studies program, wrote in a 2019 essay in *World Literature Today*:

> I heard about the occupation when I went to the Native American Studies office at Berkeley the next morning. I had driven my cab until 1 AM that morning and had not heard any news about it. When I got to the office, everyone was in a frenzy. So all those who could fit into my car crammed in and we headed for the San Francisco American Indian Center. When we got there the place was a zoo, with all kinds of people milling around. It stayed that way until midnight. After the frenzy and excitement died down, we started planning a serious occupation of the island.

What was clear to all of the potential occupiers of Alcatraz, especially Richard Oakes and LaNada, was that for a takeover to be successful, they had to be better prepared and in larger numbers. Recruiting more Indians was vital. For the next two weeks, Richard went up and down the coast, visiting colleges and universities that had Native American students. On those campuses and in the Indian bars in the city of Los Angeles, Richard found plenty of enthusiasm. The University of California, Los Angeles (UCLA) for example, proved to be very fruitful for finding volunteers. In general, Native people were excited by the newspaper and TV accounts of the November 9 attempts, which presented something positive regarding Indians in the news.

The Indians of All Tribes set a new date: November 20. It was still close enough to build on the momentum of the first attempts and far enough away for the island's caretakers and the Coast Guard to be less on guard.

There was another good thing about that date. Adam Nordwall had rubbed some of the student activists the wrong way by presenting himself as the leader of any plans to occupy the island. As LaNada explained in her book *Native Resistance*: "The U.C. Berkeley students had previously been warned by our mentors, Stella Leach and Belva Cottier, who told us to be careful of Adam Nordwall because he has a reputation as a publicity seeker using the 'Indian cause' to promote his own agenda." On November 20, Adam would be out of town at a conference for the newly formed National Indian Education Association.

Adam felt that the resentment some felt toward him was the result of a generational rift between himself and the more youthful occupiers—since he was thirty-nine at the time of the occupation. However, as Kent Blansett notes, "There are no direct quotes nor any evidence in the historical record that anyone in the IAT targeted elders . . . Richard himself was twenty-seven and never had any issue with elders . . . One of the first actions by IAT was to host a conference of elders."

Adam admits that he was a self-proclaimed showboat, which probably was a factor in the way the Native students viewed him. Still, in the months that followed, Adam worked tirelessly to gain favorable publicity for the IAT (Indians of All Tribes) and raise money for their support. Although he loved the fame that accrued to him, Adam never earned a penny from his efforts. In fact, the termite extermination business that was his livelihood went almost totally neglected.

The three ships that would carry the second group of occupiers did not leave from the main pier in San Francisco. Just off the first exit north of the San Francisco Bay Golden Gate Bridge was the Sausalito Yacht Harbor. It held country club–style yachts but also a collection of houseboats and outdated sailing vessels, jokingly referred to as the "Sausalito Navy."

Tim Findley had introduced the Indians of All Tribes to the Sausalito Navy. One of Tim's friends, Peter Bowen, owned a thirty-two-foot motorsailer, the *Seaweed*, that was a step up in class from the rest of the Sausalito Navy's boats. Bowen was the first to agree to ferry people across to Alcatraz. With the help of his friend Brooks Townes, two more boats were arranged. The second boat was the *Odin II*, owned by Bowen's friend Bob Teft. The third was run by eighteen-year-old Mary Crowley. Knowing she only had a strong sense of social justice and knew how to sail, Brooks Townes had called her with the idea of helping a group of Indians take over Alcatraz. She'd loved the idea and quickly arranged to borrow a thirty-foot sailboat.

On the night of November 20, the Indians met Peter

Bowen at a bar known as the "No Name" and then were escorted down to the water to board those three boats.

Dean Chavers had used his cab to bring some of the would-be invaders to Sausalito. He was already on Bowen's sailboat when Richard Oakes came over to him.

Oakes had remembered they needed someone to remain on the mainland and take charge of their press office. Dean, a Vietnam veteran who was older than many of the other students and also known to be a good organizer, would be the best person for that. His first job would be to start notifying the media. It made sense. So, taking another member of their group with him, Chavers turned around to do just that.

At least sixty of the Indians of All Tribes set out on those three boats, leaving thirty or more on the dock to be ferried over in a second run. The would-be occupiers were well-stocked with food, sleeping bags, and other equipment for a long stay. As they quietly crossed the bay, they saw that lights were on all over the island. Had someone alerted the authorities? Was it a sign that their landing would be prevented by armed guards? Would they be intercepted by the Coast Guard?

Although those lights had been turned on to discourage further Indian incursions, no one was watching. The Indians of All Tribes met no resistance at all in either their crossing or their landing. The boats slid alongside a water barge and tied up. Despite the unsteady footing, everybody managed to make their way safely across the barge and onto the land. The only person who fell in the water was Brooks Townes,

Landing party of occupiers being dropped off on Alcatraz

who was later described as rocketing out of the chilly water as soon as he hit it. Soon, sleeping bags in hand, the occupiers began making their way from the water barge toward the tunnel that led into the island. They kept a close watch for guards, but none were to be seen. Finally, as they neared the caretaker's shack at the far end of the dock, the lights suddenly switched on and a small man, Glenn Dodson—the only person then guarding the island—came running out.

"Mayday! Mayday!" he was yelling. "The Indians have landed."

Richard Oakes shouted back a loud "Whaaat?"

Then one of the students began to laugh. As others of the invaders joined in, Glenn Dodson began to smile. The student then strolled across the dock and wrapped one arm around the little man's shoulders in a friendly hug.

It would be hard to imagine a more peaceful—or ludicrous—takeover of any part of the United States by any group of invaders in history.

Before long, more tour guide than a guard, Dodson began to show his new friends around the island, pointing out the best places for them to spend the night.

They quickly discovered, as had the others who spent

Joe Bill with his arm around caretaker Glenn Dodson in the guard shack

that one night of November 9 on the island, that the facilities were in terrible shape. Since the closing of the prison, aside from the working lighthouse, there had been virtually no upkeep. Some of the island's buildings had electric power and were in fairly decent shape—such as the several-stories-tall apartment building that had housed prison staff. But others, including the immense cellblock that stretched across the island, were uncared for and falling into decay. Abandoned vehicles sat rusting. The only source of potable water was from the barge they had docked alongside of, used to bring drinking water from the mainland. Some places were literal fire hazards. Concrete was crumbling. They had to be careful where they stepped. And on the entire island, there were only three working toilets.

But, before long, the more than eighty occupiers all had found places for the night and settled in. A fire was going in the fireplace in the warden's house, people were sitting around swapping stories and singing traditional songs, and spirits were high. They'd done it!

All of the college student occupiers had agreed to a policy of nonviolence. LaNada Means was a veteran of this kind of action from her year of student protests at Berkeley. Richard Oakes had the examples of the White Roots of Peace and the actions that had taken place the year before at Akwesasne. Like LaNada and Richard, the other student occupiers believed in and had seen the results of nonviolence. It was agreed that passive resistance was what they would all practice. Unlike later Native American resistance events—such as the occupation of Wounded Knee in South Dakota—there were no guns among the occupiers. In fact, LaNada told me in a 2022 interview, she stopped using the name Means because of her disagreements with her former brother-in-law Russell Means about the decision made by AIM to use guns in their planned action at Wounded Knee in South Dakota. "People are going to get killed," she told them. "What would you know? You're just a woman," was the reply she got. "No weapons and none wanted" was one of the rules enforced on Alcatraz.

Now, as the occupiers sat around the fire, they just had to wait for the dawn to see what it would bring.

As luck would have it, Richard Nixon's White House found out about the Alcatraz takeover early on November 21 when Leonard Garment, the special counsel to the president, received this message on his news ticker: "Indians Seize Alcatraz."

The federal agency with authority over the abandoned island was the GSA, the government services administration. The GSA has always been responsible for government buildings, whether in active use or not. Its newly appointed director, Richard Kunzig, had also received word of the invasion. When Garment called him, Kunzig told the special counsel he was going to take care of the problem. Kunzig had already lined up a group of well-armed federal marshals to storm the island and remove the Indians by noon the next day—by whatever means necessary.

That was not what Garment or Nixon wanted to hear. That kind of confrontation, in an area already in the news because of the past year's student activism and the militancy of the Black Panthers, might ignite a powder keg. Garment ordered Kunzig, in the name of the White House, to halt his plans for a counter invasion. Kunzig was not happy but realized he was overruled. After considering peaceful options, the two men agreed that the regional administrator of the GSA in San Francisco should go to Alcatraz and talk with the Indians. That man was Tom Hannon, known for his easygoing and friendly style.

What no one in the government realized was that the Indians were one step ahead of them in contacting the GSA. As soon as the three boats had reached the island the night before, their legal representatives, R. Corbin Houchins and

Aubrey Grossman, had spoken to Hannon. Both of them were brilliant lawyers and had experience in labor and civil rights struggles.

Although Hannon, as representative of the government, was not empowered to concede to their demands of turning the island over to the Indians of All Tribes, both he and the occupiers' lawyers agreed that they needed to find a peaceful solution.

Meanwhile, as news of the occupation spread, boats began going to the island. Some were curiosity seekers while others brought food and blankets to support the Indian cause. So much boat traffic developed that a small fleet of Coast Guard cutters began to patrol the area between the mainland and Alcatraz in the week that followed. They were there not just as a blockade but also to try to prevent mid-water collisions.

Accompanied by the two lawyers, Tom Hannon made his way to the island around four o'clock in the afternoon on November 21. He was met by Richard Oakes and a fellow student, Al Miller, acting spokespersons for the Indians of All Tribes. After an hour of negotiation, a compromise was reached. A supply boat would be permitted to land the next morning, but the Indians had to leave at the end of that day. Oakes agreed to go back to the mainland to discuss things with the support group at the temporary Indian Center that had been relocated to a storefront after the fire. He climbed onto the Coast Guard cutter. But as he did so, Grossman, sleeping bag in his arms, hopped off to join the occupiers as their resident legal counsel.

CHAPTER 9

A FIRST THANKSGIVING

One of the first things the occupiers did the night of the November 20 takeover was to set up security posts throughout the island. The purpose was to keep the Coast Guard and any other government forces from invading. Despite that uncertainty, spirits were high. Before long, an all-night 49er—an impromptu celebration where people sang good-natured songs to the beat of the powwow drum—was underway around a bonfire fueled by the scrap lumber scattered around the island.

Although some have described the Indian invasion as roughly planned, it was far from that. The student occupiers and members of the Bay Area Indian community, working together at the new makeshift Indian Center, had made careful plans to sustain the community being created on the prison island. There was a mainland Indians of All Tribes office, in space provided by Dorothy Lonewolf Miller, a Blackfeet doctor. By early in the morning of November 21, Dean Chavers was barraging the media with one press release after another from that office.

A bank account had been set up, lawyers had been arranged, including one whose job would be to represent individual occupiers. (They also had Native American lawyers in Washington, D.C., who had the ears of legislators and would influence later decisions made by the administration of President Richard Nixon.) Further, a strategy for providing supplies had been put in place. Within a day after the takeover, boats were venturing out to bring provisions. Some had been chartered by the Indians of All Tribes. Even more were local people who wanted to help, sometimes sailing just close enough to toss blankets and bags of food up onto the Alcatraz dock.

For a few days, the Coast Guard attempted to intercept any boats bringing supplies. Those attempts were largely unsuccessful. There were so many that the Coast Guard lacked the resources to stop them all. And even those who were stopped received nothing more than the equivalent of a traffic ticket. A makeshift supply area was also created by the occupiers themselves on the steep rocky cliff on a part of the island away from the pier. A series of ladders were fastened together so that supplies could be brought up, passed from hand to hand in a human chain. Before many days had passed, the Coast Guard gave up its blockade.

Meanwhile, the Indians of All Tribes had very specific ideas about what would be done with Alcatraz. As Kent Blansett explained in his brilliant biography of Richard Oakes, *A Journey to Freedom*:

> The island would host a center for Native American studies with a traveling university; an American Indian spiritual center to practice native religion not yet protected by the federal government; an Indian center of ecology to formulate conservatory plans; an Indian training school, complete with a center for traditional arts and crafts; a native restaurant; and an economic school to study ways to increase employment and standards of living. Finally, their

proclamation called for the creation of an American Indian museum to expose the true history of Native America.

The November 21 deadline to vacate the island came and went without any of the eighty occupiers leaving. More days passed, and work details and cooking areas were set up. Gradually, the island was being made more livable again.

On Tuesday, November 25, a thanksgiving event took place on Alcatraz. On the one hand, it was ironic. The American holiday of Thanksgiving, a celebration of colonialism, has long been a complicated one for Native Americans, who sometimes call it the "Day of Mourning."

The U.S. celebration of Thanksgiving, on the third Thursday in November, is commonly believed to date to 1621, the year a group of Wampanoag people and Plymouth colonists shared an autumn harvest feast. Much of the food was brought to the feast by the Wampanoags. Further, that English colony had survived only because of direct help from the Wampanoags, especially from a man named Squanto, who showed the colonists how to grow corn, beans, and squash. Squanto was a fluent speaker of English. He'd been taken as a slave to

Europe and lived there for several years before finding his way back to his homeland. The tradition of thanksgiving feasts in the fall then began to be practiced in various colonies and states. However, the national holiday of Thanksgiving was not created until 1863, during the American Civil War. That was when President Abraham Lincoln, seeking ways to bring the warring states back together, proclaimed Thanksgiving as a national holiday to be celebrated every November.

Sadly, after initially living peacefully with their Indigenous neighbors, the Pilgrims and other white colonists eventually started a series of wars designed to gain Native land and drive out the original people. Those conflicts decimated the Native nations of New England, including the former allies of the Pilgrims, the Wampanoag. Those New England wars and the ones that followed—designed to displace or wipe out Indigenous people all across the continent—are why many American Indians today refer to the Thanksgiving holiday as a Day of Mourning.

On the other hand, ceremonially giving thanks is an ancient practice among many tribal nations—and not just for the harvest festival. Among Richard Oakes's own Haudenosaunee people, there are numerous thanksgiving festivals,

Participants at the thanksgiving event of November 25

such as the Thanks to the Maple when the sap begins to run in late winter, the Bean Festival, and the Green Corn Festival. There is also the tradition of the Thanksgiving Address, "the Words Before All Others," spoken ceremoniously at the start of any gathering, in which every part of Creation, from Mother Earth to the distant stars, is acknowledged and thanked.

It was an Indigenous sort of thanksgiving that took place that day on Alcatraz. Hundreds of people came, most of them Native American. Instead of Indians bringing food to white Pilgrims, turkeys and an abundance of other foods were donated to the occupying Indians by white Americans. The Bratskeller Restaurant in San Francisco had announced it would deliver a cooked dinner to everyone on the island. The Trident, a restaurant owned by the famous folk-singing group The Kingston Trio, also cooked dozens of turkeys and sent them to Alcatraz. Other restaurants and individuals donated so many turkeys that more than one person who attended that first thanksgiving powwow said there were turkeys everywhere.

Everyone was welcome, but the number of Native Americans—as many as four hundred—far outnumbered all the others who took part in that day of celebration. It was, in the memories of many, the highest point of the Alcatraz takeover. The sound of drums and traditional songs echoed across the Rock, bouncing off the unforgiving concrete walls of the cellblock.

Among those who came to that hope-filled gathering were relatives of Clarence Carnes—the Choctaw Kid who had been both the youngest person ever sent to Alcatraz and the last Indian to live on the island until the Indians of All

Tribes takeover. Although Clarence was still living, he was also still in prison, having been transferred to Leavenworth in January 1963. His release on parole back to Oklahoma would not happen until October of that year. But his mother, Alice Carnes, and his two sisters were longtime San Francisco residents, active in the Native community. Adam Nordwall described Alice as "a kind and gentle Choctaw woman from Oklahoma who had been a very valued member of our Ladies Club in the United Council." He and others who knew her wondered what thoughts were going through her head as she set foot on that liberated island that had been her son's place of captivity and exile for so many years.

Adam was one of the first to arrive on that day of celebration. Arrayed in full regalia and standing at the prow of a tugboat, he raised his arms high over his head in triumph as the ship touched the pier. Some of the student occupiers of the island were amused—or disgusted—by the way he seemed to take credit for everything that had happened. That thanksgiving gathering was the first time in 1969 that Adam set foot on Alcatraz during the occupation. He did not spend a single night there during the nineteen months of the occupation. However, his dedication to the cause was played out in his media connections and his fundraising on the mainland. And other members of his family, including his children and his brothers, would all spend time on the island.

It would be impossible to recount all the stories that took place over the next year and a half. Not just hundreds but thousands of American

Adam Nordwall (Fortunate Eagle) addressing the press.

Indians made their way to the island during the occupation. Many came to spend only a night or two before leaving, while others spent weeks or even months. Most were deeply inspired by what they saw. Despite continuing orders from the government for the Native occupiers to leave, the number of Indians coming to the island increased. Like the Statue of Liberty was for European immigrants on the East Coast, for American Indians, Alcatraz became a beacon and a symbol of freedom, a kind of freedom they had not known for centuries.

Sage Road Traveler Longoria (Caddo) Nation (left) and Diana Vargas (right) waiting for the ferry to Alcatraz, May 30, 1970

CHAPTER 10

THOSE WHO CAME

Alcatraz became a place of pilgrimage, an Indian mecca for Native people from hundreds of tribes. Some were there for a day or two while others arrived with the intention of staying. It's estimated that the average daily number of Indians on the island who were "permanent," that is, there to stay as long as possible, was about fifty. However, it was common on any given day—especially in the first months of the takeover—for hundreds to be there.

Among those who arrived for that first thanksgiving was a twenty-six-year-old Santee Dakota man who had been living in Los Angeles. At the age of seventeen, he had joined the Navy and served from 1963 to 1967. Following that, he had gone to San Bernadino Community College, where he'd studied radio and broadcasting. Before the month was over, he and his pregnant wife, Felicia Ordonez, had moved to Alcatraz, where their son, Wovoka, was born in 1970. This man was John Trudell, and he would end up being one of the longest staying and most crucial Native inhabitants of the island. Not long after his arrival, he became the voice of what was called Radio Free Alcatraz. On December 22, KPFA-FM in Berkeley—with the support of the Pacifica Foundation—began providing the occupiers with fifteen minutes of airtime every evening at 7:15 P.M. The show's title was a play on Radio Free Europe, the U.S. government's programs beamed to the then Communist nations of Europe behind the Iron Curtain. Each evening, Trudell interviewed residents of the island, reported on Indian affairs, and showcased Native elders telling traditional stories. WBAI in New York City, affiliated with KPFA, also carried the program, which reached an audience of more than one hundred thousand listeners.

Soon after that thanksgiving, another significant person in the history of the takeover arrived, a Sac and Fox woman named Grace Thorpe. Grace was the daughter of the famous

Grace Thorpe (Sac and Fox) with John Trudell (Santee Sioux) on Radio Alcatraz

Native American athlete Jim Thorpe. After hearing news reports of the Indian occupation, Grace left her job selling advertising and real estate, put her furniture into storage, and spent her savings to travel to the island and remain there for much of the rest of the occupation. Joined by her daughter Dagmar, Grace was media savvy, working on press releases and appearing frequently on Radio Free Alcatraz. After the decision was made by the island council to restrict residency to Natives, it was Grace who handled writing diplomatic letters to white supporters who wished to join the occupation, thanking them while explaining that the island was for Indians only, "our first free land since the white man came."

Another whose words became part of the island's history was Peter Blue Cloud. Like Richard Oakes, Peter was Mohawk and a former ironworker. He was from Kahnawake, a reservation not far from Richard's Akwesasne. The two became close friends on Alcatraz and often would be heard conversing with each other in the Mohawk language. A poet with strong ties to such beat generation figures as Gary Snyder, Blue Cloud created and edited an *Indians of All Tribes Newsletter*. He later published a small anthology called *Alcatraz Is Not an Island*. His introductory words in the book clearly express one of the aims of the occupiers:

Dear America, the people: We present these documents and thoughts concerning the Indian occupation of Alcatraz in the hope that a better understanding may be reached between peoples of various cultural backgrounds and traditions.

It was Peter who handled the shortwave radio that was a primary means of rapid communication (decades before cell phones) between the island and the Indian Center on the mainland.

In the early days of the occupation, almost anyone had been welcome to stay or at least visit overnight. At first, it didn't matter if they were Indian or non-Native. That gradually changed when visitors began taking advantage of the hospitality they were offered or tried to bring some aspects of the hippie lifestyle, drugs in particular, to the island.

There were also white Evangelists who made themselves unwelcome by stating their intent to convert the "pagan Indians." Not only was that insulting to Native Americans following traditional ways, most of the Indians of All Tribes had been brought up in one Christian faith or another.

A long list of celebrities from that period came and spent brief periods on Alcatraz. Jane Fonda and Marlon Brando were two of the Hollywood movie stars who were committed activists and risked their reputations to provide moral and financial support to the Indians of All Tribes. Fonda took part in press conferences for Alcatraz, as well as demonstrations for other Native causes on the West Coast. Dick Gregory, the Black comedian and civil rights activist, donated a large sum of money. Actor Anthony Quinn, then starring in a movie about a drunken Indian, visited Alcatraz, but apparently he did so primarily to gain publicity for his new film. The popular rock group Creedence Clearwater Revival put on a benefit concert and donated the money to the Indians of All Tribes. It was used to purchase a boat, formerly called the *Bass Tub II* and rechristened the *Clearwater*. Although the aging vessel was not in great shape, it was in constant use ferrying people back and forth to the island and bringing supplies before it sank a year later while tied up at the Alcatraz dock. Some felt its sinking was a result of sabotage, though others said they were surprised it kept floating for as long as it did.

TV and media people were constantly coming to the island to film, photograph, and write stories about what was happening there. Between November 20, 1969, and January 1970, the *San Francisco Chronicle* and the *San Francisco Examiner* published more than 125 articles about Alcatraz. Many were written by Tim Findlay, who continued to support the Indians of All Tribes cause. But it was not just the local media who covered the occupation. National and international coverage was taking place on a daily basis. LaNada Means would end up with her picture on the cover of *Ramparts* magazine—

LaNada Means stands beneath her Ramparts photo (top right) in 2019 at a National Park Service exhibit called "Red Power on Alcatraz, Perspectives 50 Years Later."

one of the most popular countercultural publications of the period. A photo of her posing in front of a wall with BETTER RED THAN DEAD graffitied in crimson paint accompanied an article about the takeover. It was one of the few cases where the central role of Native women in the occupation was some-what acknowledged. The process of erasing the presence and

OF ALL TRIBES

Belva Cottier and a young Chicano man on Alcatraz Island, May 30, 1970

contributions of women was common. Even today, there is still a tendency to see men, not women, as leaders—including in Native cultures where women have always played central roles.

By early December, the occupiers decided that a governing body of some sort was needed, a board of directors or council. Its dual role would be to deal with the press and the government and to make decisions. The seven men chosen to sit on that council were Ed Castillo, Ross Harden, Al Miller, Bob Nelford, Richard Oakes, Dennis Turner, and

James Vaughn. They were all young and most were college students, with the exception of Castillo, who had taken a leave from his job as a UCLA instructor.

Richard Oakes was chosen to act as spokesperson for the council. With his cinematic good looks and eloquence, he was the perfect person for that role. He played it gracefully and with an easy sense of humor. However, because of that visibility, he was often described by the white press as the leader, the "Chief," or even the "Mayor of Alcatraz." Before long, some of the Indian occupiers grew uncomfortable with that. The idea of one person being elevated above all others went against their belief in the communal nature of the enterprise.

Ed Castillo was chosen to be the head of security. As a relatively short individual with a slight build, being the head of security was not the best role for Castillo to play. After a number of tense run-ins with larger and stronger Indian men, he resigned.

Meanwhile, the council was meeting on a regular basis, sometimes several times a day, to address whatever issues came up. Everyone could attend the meetings and everyone had a voice, making decisions not by a majority vote but in the traditional way by reaching a consensus all could accept.

It was also agreed that every ninety days a new council would be elected.

Donations of money, food, and used clothing (including such things as high heels and cocktail dresses—not really suitable for life on the island) continued to pour in. A center, with the sign ALCATRAZ RECEIVING DEPOT, was set up on Pier 40 on the mainland where donated materials could be stored and Indians going to the island could wait for boats. Joseph Morris, a Blackfeet Indian who was a member of the local longshoreman's union, had helped acquire that space for free. A dedicated group of volunteers, including Dean Chavers and Earl Livermore, worked long hours staging the boats' runs to the island, loaded with people and supplies.

Lawyers had been working behind the scenes. Negotiations were proceeding on a regular basis between the Indians of All Tribes and the U.S. government. The proposal that Alcatraz be legally ceded to the Indians of All Tribes was not something the government was willing to accept. But the idea of an armed invasion was also something the U.S. government did not yet have the stomach to order.

Many of the men who came to the island brought with them useful mechanical and construction skills. Work on

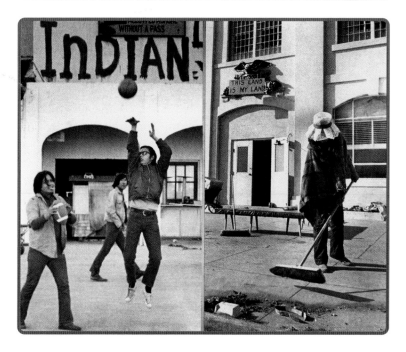

Everyday life on Alcatraz

making the aging facilities more livable went on daily. Trash was cleared away. The dock was repaired. Indian mechanics got some of the abandoned trucks back into running order. Before long, working generators and several dozen toilets were in operation.

However, the island was still and always would be without its own source of water. It was only regular shipments to fill the water barge tied to the Alcatraz docks that kept that essential life support available. The GSA had the power to cut off phone service and the electric supply to the island at any time. However, for most of the nineteen months of the occupation, that was not done. The major reason had nothing to do with the Indian occupiers. The one structure on the island that had been kept in good running order was the Alcatraz lighthouse. Each night, its beam cut across the bay and was a major aid for navigating those waters. Without electricity, it would go dark.

Throughout it all, the tactic taken by the Alcatraz Indians was a simple one. They were there. They were not going to go away. Constant attention from the press, and visits from one celebrity after another, made success seem possible.

However, behind all the support, behind all of the organization, there was a ripple of discontent. Whenever someone is too much in the public eye, they may be criticized. There's an old saying among the Haudenosaunee: "The skin of a chief must be seven thumbs thick." When you are recognized as a leader, people will snipe at you. Oakes and others who assumed positions of authority on the island always had to deal with that.

Those on the island were a community of equals, making decisions by consensus. That they were "from all tribes" was a source of strength. However, it was sometimes a cause of dissension. Tribal loyalty was more important to some than was pan-Indianism. By mid-January 1970, parts of the cell-block and other buildings had been claimed in the name of one tribal nation or another, with signs on doorways reading LODGE OF THE CHEYENNE and POMO ROOM! DO NOT DISTURB. Some were meant jokingly. Others were more serious.

Alcohol, a source of conflict in everyday Native city life, was forbidden. The image of the drunken Indian was something that the Indians of All Tribes wanted to avoid. Although it didn't always prevent the use of other illegal substances, such as marijuana, the policy of sobriety was enforced.

After that first magnificent thanksgiving feast, word spread that Alcatraz was a place where Indians could be free of government control, fed, and housed. That resulted in some people coming to the island as freeloaders. Some were not even Indians. The original Native college student occupiers became disgusted. As Oakes put it: "Our biggest problems are freelance photographers and the hippies. They stay and eat up our stores and then leave."

OF ALL TRIBES

The 1960s saw the birth of New Age ideas and practices. In some cases, these ideas involved "plastic medicine men"—white people taking Indian names, engaging in supposedly authentic ceremonies, and setting themselves up as spiritual guides (for a price). These white so-called shamans had few or no genuine connections to the traditions they claimed to represent. There were even a few actual Native Americans who took that route. One such Native "medicine man," accompanied by his white followers, came to Alcatraz. Before he could disembark, he was told they were not welcome and were sent back to the mainland.

Eventually, only real Indians would be allowed to stay on the island. And if they wanted to remain, they could not be freeloaders. They had to abide by the rules and help in whatever way they could. There was always more than enough to do, from the mundane jobs of cooking, cleaning up garbage, and making repairs, to bookkeeping, decision-making, and dealing with the media. Whatever skill someone had was put to good use throughout the nineteen months. That was especially true of Stella Leach.

On November 22, the Colville Lakota activist who had been an advisor to LaNada and the other UC Berkeley

Stella Leach (Colville-Sioux)

Indian students moved to Alcatraz. Two of Stella's six adult children, David Leach and Gary Leach, both Vietnam veterans, were already there. David had been part of the original landing party of eighty-nine people on November 20. In addition to being a strong-minded elder, Stella was also a licensed practical nurse with a certificate from Laney College. In 1964, she'd helped form the first All-Indian Well Baby Clinic in the Bay Area. Given a three-month leave of absence from her employer, Dr. David Tepper, she set up a health clinic on the ground floor of the former employees' apartment building. Her staff included two other Native women, both nurses, Dorothy Lonewolf Miller (Blackfeet) and Jennie R. Joe (Dine), and Dr. Tepper himself, who volunteered his services once a week. It was not an easy job. Conditions on the island, where it was cold and often rainy, were unsanitary. Without running water, heat, and electricity, people were often sick and suffering from the stomach problems commonly known as "Geronimo's Revenge." But Stella soldiered through it all, and after her three-month leave ended, she stayed on for another six months.

There were also a few Natives who came to Alcatraz who did not practice nonviolence. On more than one occasion, Richard Oakes and others had to break up fights and escort offenders off the Rock.

The American Indian Movement (AIM) was just starting to gain attention in 1970. It had been founded in the Minneapolis/St. Paul area to try to protect Indians from police profiling. AIM had not been involved in any way with the takeover of the island. In early 1970, though, a group of AIM members finally did come to Alcatraz. They were there not just to provide moral support but also to take advantage of what they saw as an opportunity to gain more visibility and publicity for their own organization. As they were being shown around, the leader of the delegation said, "You guys did a good job, you took it over, and now we'll take it and run it from here." Richard's forceful reply, in colorful language, was that they should get off Alcatraz or else. The AIM delegation left and never returned.

By the early months of 1970, most of the original student occupiers were leaving, going back to the mainland to begin a new semester of classes. If they hadn't returned, they would have lost their enrollments and been unable to continue their educations. Remaining on Alcatraz would have been not only difficult but also more of a sacrifice than they wanted to make.

LaNada was not among those who left. Nor did she give up her college plans. Despite being a single mother and maintaining a quiet but always deeply involved presence on the island, she managed to balance keeping up with her studies with her work on the island. Every morning, one or two boats left Alcatraz to carry people to the mainland, and every evening, those boats or other ones would bring people back to the Rock. "I would hitchhike off the docks at Alcatraz," LaNada wrote, "and catch a sailboat or a speedboat to the Berkeley Marina . . . go to my apartment at the university college, clean up, and then I would check in on my classes."

Things, however, were not going as well for Richard Oakes. By early January 1970, he was being constantly criticized by those who were envious of his media stardom. He was even accused of taking some of the checks sent by well-wishers for his own personal use. The accusations were baseless but hurtful.

Annie Oakes, herself a very strong individual, was feeling discouraged. It wasn't just because of the petty jealousy and the sniping at her husband. She wanted to do more for her own California Indian community, the Pomo Nation, which was involved in its own struggles against the government.

She and Richard and their children were residing in one of the two former employees' apartment buildings on the lower level of the island. It was better than camping out or living in one of the old cellblocks where some people insisted on staying. But Alcatraz was still a cold, hard place.

From the first day of the occupation to the last, there were always families with children among the Indians of

All Tribes. When that first group of ninety or more arrived on November 20 and were unpacking their things, out from under a pile of sleeping bags came crawling a girl. It was Annie and Richard's thirteen-year-old daughter, Yvonne, who had stowed away. That same night, LaNada, accompanied by her younger sister Claudene, brought her two-and-a-half-year-old son. There are pictures of her holding him as the boat she was on approached Alcatraz.

Having children on the island was important for several reasons. It made it clear that the takeover was a family event, not just a bunch of dangerous activists. Having families on the island made it feel more like a real community. It also made it less likely that the government would attempt to remove the Indians of All Tribes in any violent fashion. There had been so much in the news that darkened the image of the United States, including massacres of civilians by American soldiers in Vietnam. The public face of dragging women and children off the island was not something the U.S. government wanted.

A freedom school was set up on the island to help the children of Alcatraz keep up with their education. The first class of twelve students was taught by Douglas Remington

Two Indian children play on abandoned Department of Justice equipment on Alcatraz Island, 1970.

and Linda Arayando. Remington, a twenty-four-year-old Southern Ute, had a bachelor's degree in English and a master's degree in theater arts. Arayando, a Creek, was a twenty-one-year-old senior at Berkeley majoring in social science. Called the Big Rock School, classes were held in the assembly hall of the main cellblock. In addition to the standard syllabus in reading, writing, and arithmetic, they also studied Native American history and culture. Standard California school system texts were used as well as material provided by the Head Start Program at St John the Evangelist Episcopal Church in San Francisco. Ranging from first to sixth grade, it never received full accreditation. However, the school officials in San Francisco agreed not to penalize any parents if their children missed school in the city. A parallel school focusing on such traditional crafts as beadwork, wood carving, and leatherwork was run by Earl Livermore (Blackfeet), the director of the San Francisco American Indian Center. A nursery school for the very young children whose parents were busy with other tasks was set up in the cellblock's former office quarters and was run by Dagmar Thorpe and Lu Trudell.

Things on Alcatraz were not perfect, but they were moving along. Then a terrible tragedy took place.

Richard Oakes's daughter, Yvonne, flashes the Victory sign. Richard is at left.

CHAPTER 11

AFTER THE FALL

In early January 1970, Richard and Annie left the island to do some business on the mainland. By then, two months into the occupation, it was common practice for people to go back and forth between the island and the mainland.

Instead of blockading the island, the Coast Guard was now providing help. For example, when someone was injured on the island—which happened far too often, as a result both of the deteriorating nature of its infrastructure and of the occasional fight—it was usually the Coast Guard that would take them from Alcatraz to get medical help in the city.

Richard and Annie left thirteen-year-old Yvonne to babysit her younger siblings. It was not unusual for parents to let their children run free, riding their bikes or exploring the island. Trusting children to make good decisions on their own is a common cultural practice in Native communities. That day, a few hours after Annie and Richard left, Yvonne began playing tag with some of her friends. Their game took them to the stairway in the apartment building now called the Ira Hayes House in honor of the Pima Indian who helped raise the flag on Iwo Jima in World War II. The three flights of concrete stairs were steep. The railing on top was a low one. A fast runner, Yvonne was far ahead of the two boys chasing her. They heard her scream from the top of the stairs and saw her fall past them, landing headfirst on the concrete below.

One of the first to reach her was Stella Leach, who had also heard Yvonne's scream in her clinic. As Yvonne lay there, bleeding and unconscious, Stella did whatever she could to stabilize the badly injured child and prepare her to be taken to the city, where she could get the kind of emergency treatment she needed.

The Coast Guard quickly evacuated Yvonne to the mainland, and she was taken to the public health service hospital. Richard and Annie rushed there as soon as they heard the

Fog comes in over Alcatraz as an Indian woman walks toward the Ira Hayes House.

news and found their daughter still unconscious and in critical condition.

At two-thirty that afternoon, T. E. Hannon, who despite his role representing the government had become friends with the Oakes family, arrived to offer his support. While Richard was out of the room, Annie confided in Hannon that they wondered if it was more than an accident. She'd had a premonition a while before that something terrible was going to happen. Things were getting worse now on the island, she told Hannon. There was fighting and drinking and "nothing was going right." To this day, there are still unanswered questions about what caused Yvonne's fall.

On January 8, despite the best round-the-clock care from the hospital, whose administrators had assured Richard and Annie that the hospital would absorb any costs, Yvonne passed away.

Richard pleaded with Hannon to not forcibly remove the Indians of All Tribes from Alcatraz. But Richard's role on the island was done. After less than two months on Alcatraz, he, Annie, and their family left and never returned to live there again.

"You guys," Richard told Al Miller, "do what you can with it. I don't have the heart for it anymore."

The job of representing to the public the Indian side of the story of the occupation of Alcatraz, which was beginning to look to some in the media like a sinking ship, would have to pass to other hands.

After Yvonne's tragic death, some of those in the press who had supported the occupation now began to criticize the Indians of All Tribes. Tim Findley wrote two scathing articles comparing life on Alcatraz to that in *Lord of the*

Flies, a grim novel in which a group of English boys stranded on an island turn into bloodthirsty savages. But the story of Indian control of the former prison island was far from over.

With her usual determination, Stella Leach was one of those who was ready to take up the challenge after Richard's departure. Respected for her role in running the clinic, she was chosen to be one of the seven members of the new Alcatraz board of directors. She also was selected to be the spokesperson for the board, speaking both to the media and with the government.

It also helped that she had the support of the Thunderbirds, a group of young Indian men who had been invited to the island to handle security, now that Richard, who had always used his charisma and his reputation as a street fighter to defuse potential conflicts, was gone. Though known as a street gang by the mainland police and sometimes in conflict with the Samoan community in the Mission District, the Thunderbirds were not regarded by most Native people in the Bay Area as a threat. Described jokingly as "the Indian biker gang without bikes because they could not afford them," many were Vietnam veterans. LaNada's brother Dwayne Boyer had organized them. Dressed in army fatigues and wearing red headbands and armbands, they were a very visible—and sometimes controversial—presence on the island.

Negotiations between the Indians of All Tribes and government officials continued without pause after Richard's departure. LaNada had written the planning grant for the creation of a university, an Indian museum, and an environmental center on the island. She helped find an architecture firm, MacDonald Architects, that volunteered to create the design for the project. She had met and befriended Edgar Cahn, a Washington lawyer whose book, *Our Brother's Keeper*, about the bleak conditions on reservations, had just been published. Through Cahn and his wife, Jean, who was also a lawyer, LaNada had met with Browning Pipestem (Otoe/Missouria/Osage), a Native lawyer working with a high-profile D.C. law firm. Pipestem agreed to be their lawyer in Washington, pro bono—at no cost. The Cahns and Pipestem were well connected, working with such people as Sargent Shriver, who had helped found the Peace Corps and lead Johnson's war on poverty legislation. They gave the Indians of All Tribes an influential direct link to the White House.

Even though those plans for the development of Alcatraz

were not agreed to by the government and despite an undercurrent of dissention on the island, LaNada and others worked to keep the dream alive until the end of the occupation.

While many in the federal government agreed that helping Indians was a good idea, developing an Indian complex on Alcatraz was thought to be the wrong approach. The location was the problem. Maintaining anything on Alcatraz was difficult and would be extremely costly. The federal prison had been shut down because of the challenges of maintaining it there.

A secret removal plan code-named Operation Parks was drawn up by the government. The island came under close surveillance by the FBI. Spotters with high-power telescopes in San Francisco were based in tall buildings near the bay, and low-flying planes took photographs of the occupiers. However, Operation Parks was meant only to be a backup if negotiations failed.

At the urging of the government, a new Native organization was formed. All the Natives of the Bay Area, including Adam Nordwall and others in the older generation that the government hoped would be easier to deal with, were included. The Bay Area Native American Council (BANAC) was its name. A $50,000 grant (equivalent to about $370,000 today) to fight poverty was offered to BANAC, with the stipulation that the Alcatraz takeover would end. What the government negotiators did not realize was that the new organization would support whatever decision the Indians on the island made. Although some later portrayed the short-lived BANAC as having been at odds with the Indians of All Tribes, the organization's name came from LaNada. It was not an accident that the acronym was a pun on the name of her Bannock Tribe. The grant, with its conditions of ending the occupation, was refused.

By March 1970, the government had reached its final conclusion about what to do with Alcatraz. A Golden Gate National Recreation Area, stretching nearly sixty miles along the coastline, would be created and would include the rocky island. The occupiers were approached in late March with a new proposal. If they agreed, Alcatraz Island could become a federal park dedicated to Native American history and culture. The response from the Indians of All Tribes was a firm no.

In a press conference following that decision, John Trudell stated, "All we get out of this meeting with the U.S.

government and their representatives is that they are going to continue to do as they have done in the past—which is to do our thinking for us and run things their way."

The government decided it was time to turn to action, now that talking had failed. Operation Parks was still an option but only as a last resort. A softer strategy would be tried first. At the end of May, the Coast Guard hauled away the water barge that had been the only source of water for drinking, cooking, and washing. Then the electricity and phone service were cut.

Coast Guard towing away the water barge

OF ALL TRIBES

Though it made things more difficult, the Indians of All Tribes did not give up. Water was brought on boats from the mainland, and gas-powered generators provided electricity for lights and to keep the fog horns and lighthouse working. Even though things had been made harder for them, the Indians of All Tribes kept the lighthouse operating in the interest of keeping the bay waters safe to navigate.

On Memorial Day, May 31, a powwow was celebrated on the island. Hundreds of Indians showed up for the event they called Indian Liberation Day. A Declaration of the Return of Indian Land was drafted and then written on a large tanned hide. Among other things, it refused the acceptance of money for Indian land and stated, "We announce on behalf of all Indian people, or tribes that from this day forward we shall exercise dominion and all rights of use and possession over Alcatraz Island in San Francisco Bay."

It was a moment of celebration that would be all too brief.

Tongue-in-cheek Declaration of the Return of Indian Land inscribed on animal hide, May 31, 1970

President Nixon shaking hands and meeting with American Indian leaders of the Taos Pueblo Indian Tribal Council (Blue Lake). July 8, 1970, Washington, D.C., White House, Cabinet Room.

CHAPTER 12

NIXON'S CHIEF

Although few of the Indians of All Tribes knew it, throughout their occupation until the very end, they had a sympathetic ear in Washington. The measured response the federal government would take throughout the takeover of Alcatraz Island reflected the attitude toward Indians of none other than Richard M. Nixon, the president of the United States.

In fact, President Nixon, despite his later bad reputation owing to the Watergate scandal and his resignation from the presidency, was a real friend to Indians. He did more for Native Americans in his public pronouncements and the policies he put forward and advanced than any other president in American history.

More than twenty major pieces of legislation that positively affected American Indian communities and Native culture in general came from the Nixon years. The end of termination and the restoration of federal recognition to many of the hundred terminated tribes was only one of the massive changes Nixon initiated. Relocation ended under his watch. Hundreds of thousands of acres of land were returned to Taos Pueblo and the Navajo Nation. Nixon would sign the Alaska Native Claims Settlement Act of 1970, the Indian Education Act of 1972, and the Menominee Restoration Act of 1973 and introduce the new policy of self-determination in his "Special Message to Congress On Indian affairs" in 1970. The entire direction of federal Indian policy transitioned from termination to self-determination.

In all fairness, the move toward major changes in Indian policy had actually begun before Nixon took office. Had it not been for the Vietnam War, President Lyndon B. Johnson (LBJ) might have been regarded as one of the most forward-looking chief executives in American history in terms of minority rights. His record in civil rights was far better than that of any president before him and many who followed. Domestic programs, Johnson's first love, might have defined him far differently than his image as a war maker. But the morass of the deeply unpopular war in Southeast Asia made his public image so negative that he decided not to run for reelection.

In the last year of his presidency, 1968, Johnson had made a call for Indian self-determination. All of the major pieces of legislation that would eventually end termination and relocation and open a new era of possibility for American Indians were launched by his administration that year.

It was fortunate for those policies and Native Americans in general that Richard Nixon embraced and continued them as his own when he took office. He did this despite the fact that he and President Johnson came from different political parties and that Nixon had run for office portraying himself as the opposite of LBJ and the only one who could get America out of Vietnam.

Why was Nixon so friendly to Native Americans? It wasn't a case of a romantic infatuation with Indians. It stemmed from his upbringing. Not only was he raised as a

Quaker, a religious order traditionally supportive of Indians, his football coach at Whittier College, Wallace "Chief" Newman, was Native American. Nixon learned from Newman, respected him, and saw him as a friend and lifelong mentor.

Although little-known today, Newman was an inspiring and highly successful figure. Head coach at Whittier College from 1929 to 1951, Newman was a Luiseno Indian from the La Jolla Reservation in California. As dedicated to his people and Native American rights as he was to coaching, Newman, who was tribally enrolled, would go on to be the president of the Mission Creek band of Mission Indians after his coaching career ended, and would hold that position until his tribe was terminated.

Even though Nixon, who weighed only 140 pounds in college, sat on the bench for most of the time, he saw Chief Newman as a role model. "He drilled into me," Nixon wrote, "a competitive spirit and determination to come back after you have been knocked down or after you lose. He also gave me an acute understanding that what really matters is not a man's background, his color, his race, or his religion, but only his character." Aside from his own father, Nixon said, no one taught him more than his college coach.

Nixon's personal connections with Newman lasted long after the president's college years. Newman campaigned for Nixon again and again and often appeared with him in public on the campaign trail. He served on the president's Commission on Physical Fitness and Sports and was considered for the role of Commissioner of Indian Affairs. When Nixon

Nixon's Coach Wallace "Chief" Newman (Luiseno-Mission Creek)

signed the legislation returning the sacred Blue Lake and its surrounding thousands of acres to the Taos Pueblo, he talked about the way Chief Newman had helped people through the Depression years. "I have often spoken," he said, "of the fact that one of the men that influenced me most in my college career happened to be my football coach, who was an American Indian."

So it was that when Nixon entered the presidency in

1968, he was more actively sympathetic to Native Americans than any president before him.

It's little wonder that his White House team dealt evenhandedly and patiently with the Alcatraz occupation. Nixon also had extremely good advisors when it came to Native American affairs. They were not people who thought, as had been the case for a century of federal policy, that the best thing to do for Native Americans was to absorb them into the greater American society, wiping out all traces of their languages, cultures, and Indigenous heritage.

Richard Nixon had received a tremendous mandate in both his election and his reelection, sweeping nearly every state. His popularity far exceeded that of his Democrat predecessor Lyndon Johnson or that of Hubert Humphrey and George McGovern, the two candidates who ran against him. Thus, it was much easier for him to find support in Congress for his ideas. Further, Nixon's focus—and that of the overall nation—was much more on foreign affairs than on domestic ones. Bringing a conclusion to the warfare in Southeast Asia was priority number one for his presidency and for the American electorate.

Following Nixon's lead, during the nineteen months of the Alcatraz occupation, government negotiators would treat the

Indians of All Tribes with respect and make relatively reasonable proposals to them. It was only in the last days of the takeover that the use of force would finally be put into motion.

It's also true that, although President Nixon held the awesome powers of the presidency, he was not in full control of every part of the federal government—in particular the FBI.

One thing that is now known, and was then only rumored, was that the FBI had been actively targeting domestic American political organizations for a decade and a half. A well-organized counterintelligence program, known as COINTELPRO, was begun in 1956. Its initial purpose was to monitor and neutralize the influence of the Communist Party in the United States. J. Edgar Hoover, the powerful director of the FBI, quickly reclassified the program to target such Black civil rights leaders as Dr. Martin Luther King, Jr.

By the mid-1960s, the program had vastly broadened its focus. It was now aimed at surveilling, infiltrating, discrediting, and disrupting a wide range of domestic political organizations including anti-Vietnam organizers, feminist organizations, the Nation of Islam, the Black Panther Party, environmentalist and animal rights organizations, Puerto Rican independence groups, and the American Indian Movement.

OF ALL TRIBES

According to a Senate report in 1976, the FBI's motivation was "protecting national security, preventing violence, and maintaining the existing social and political order." Many of the COINTELPRO projects were not only covert but also illegal. In the case of the Black Panther Party, its leaders were actively targeted for neutralization by being publicly humiliated, falsely charged with crimes, imprisoned, and even assassinated.

There is no doubt that the FBI was closely focused on the takeover of Alcatraz. Many of those on Alcatraz were aware of the danger from the FBI, although the extent of COINTELPRO was not yet publicly known. LaNada and others had seen what was happening to the Black Panthers. In addition to being committed to nonviolence, the Indians of All Tribes did not want to give the government the excuse to assassinate them as it had such armed Black Panther leaders as Fred Hampton. "If we'd had guns," LaNada said, "they would have killed us."

With all of the comings and goings on the island, it would have been easy for the FBI to infiltrate the Indians of All Tribes by sending in Indians (or people who pretended to be Indians) as covert operatives.

CHAPTER 13

TAKING IT BACK

On June 1, 1970, two days after the Memorial Day pow-wow and while LaNada and John Trudell were on the mainland doing a radio broadcast, fires broke out on Alcatraz. At 11 P.M., the Coast Guard sent a boat to investigate. It reported back that the east side of the island was in flames. The blaze was centered around the warden's house and the lighthouse. The Indians tried to stop the fire, but without the water barge, there was little they could do. Centered at the top and in the middle of the island, the hoses from Coast Guard boats could not reach it. Eventually, all they could do was retreat to a safe distance and let it burn.

The government blamed the fire on the Indians, saying it was perhaps the result of a smoker's dropped match. Some thought the blaze was sparked by a flare fired from a passing boat. But most of the Indians, justifiably suspicious, believed it was set by a saboteur, someone posing as a friend who was in fact a government agent. John Trudell would report on his Radio Alcatraz newscast that a boat had been seen roaring away from the island just before the fires began. The real cause of the fire, which began to turn public opinion against the Indians of All Tribes, remains unknown to this day. The gutted buildings it left behind also made living conditions even more difficult than they had been before. Tom Hannon, who had befriended Richard Oakes and his family, looked at it with some dismay. "Alcatraz," he said, was now "an island ghetto."

But it was also still an inspiration. Indians who had been on Alcatraz were beginning to take similar actions all around the nation. After leaving the island, Richard Oakes had returned to the city with Annie and their children and resumed his studies at San Francisco State, working for the Native American Studies Department and starting a scholarship fund for Indian students in Yvonne's name. The Pit River Tribe in Northern California began an action in early

June, a road blockade and encampment on land controlled by Pacific Gas and Electric (PG&E). Their aim was to reclaim 3.5 million acres, including the PG&E land, that had been taken from them by the government in 1853. Richard went there to support them and so, too, did Grace Thorpe.

But Richard's organizing for Pitt River—and almost his life—came to a sudden end. On June 11, 1970, he was in San Francisco in Warren's Bar. Richard felt at home there. It was where he'd been a bartender during his early years in the city. Like most Native bars, it was as much a place to socialize and make contacts as it was to drink. It was where he'd recruited for San Francisco State and Alcatraz. His Akwesasne Mohawk buddy Louis Mitchell and two other friends were with him. They'd just come from a meeting where, with Grace Thorpe, they had discussed plans for further actions in their Pit River campaign against PG&E.

But while his back was turned, someone came up behind Richard. He heard his name called, turned, and was struck in the head with the heavy end of a pool cue. He fell to the floor, senseless. Then his assailant, a twenty-eight-year-old Samoan man named Tommy Pritchard who'd lost a fight with Richard two months before, struck him again in the head. It happened so fast that most people missed it. Seeing his friend on the floor, Louis Mitchell thought perhaps he'd drunk too much. He and the other two men carried him home, where he was put to bed, still unconscious. The next morning, seeing how swollen his head was, Annie called an ambulance and he was taken to the hospital.

The prognosis was that the brain damage was so severe he would not survive. On June 24, he was visited by Mad Bear Anderson, the Tuscarora activist and healer. Mad Bear had rushed from his home near Niagara Falls when he heard about his friend Richard's condition. Peter Mitten, a Cayuga medicine person from Canada, was with him. The doctors said there was no hope. Richard had a life-threatening fever of 106 degrees. But they agreed it would do no harm for him to be treated traditionally. The two men prayed and burned sweet grass. Then Peter Mitten placed a special medicine into Richard's feeding tube. Almost immediately, a spot of color formed on his chest. Within an hour, his temperature dropped and his body relaxed. Gradually, over the weeks that followed, he improved. Although weak and in a wheelchair, he was able to check himself out of the hospital on August 19.

Though he could not return to his classes, Richard recovered enough in the months that followed to once again think about the struggle for Native rights. After a brief visit back east to Akwesasne in the fall of 1970, he and Annie and the children returned to the West Coast, where he began organizing other occupations with Northern California tribes, one of which led to the return of 125 acres to the Pomo Tribe where the Ya-Ka-Ama Education Center was set up.

Other Native activists who had been at Alcatraz were engaging in dozens of Indigenous protests, occupations, and fish-ins (where Indians would fish without a license claiming aboriginal treaty rights to do so), and many who initiated direct actions throughout the nation not only cited Alcatraz as an inspiration but described themselves as Indians of All Tribes.

In August 1970, a tour boat called the *Harbor Queen* was struck by an arrow shot from Alcatraz. It did not harm anyone, simply bouncing off the side of the boat. But it caused a stir and calls for the Coast Guard to end the occupation. However, John Trudell, in his nightly Radio Free Alcatraz broadcast, responded with typical dry humor. In recent weeks, they'd been bothered by boats sailing close to the island to harass and heckle the occupiers. What happened, he said, was nothing more than an attempt by someone unnamed to convince those tourist boats to keep a respectful distance. "And now," Trudell said, "with one forty-two-cent arrow, we've stopped it."

By September, however, the government had had enough. They were ready to proceed with Operation Parks. Helicopters, boats, and armed marshals were preparing the assault. Somehow, word about the plan leaked before it could be put into action. Herb Caen, a columnist with the *San Francisco Chronicle*, revealed it to the public. On Alcatraz, the Thunderbird security force used metal fuel drums to block the open spaces on the island where helicopters could land. With the element of surprise lost, the government denied the existence of Operation Parks and the invasion was canceled.

On November 9, 1970, a celebration took place recognizing the one-year anniversary of the first attempt by the Indians of All Tribes to take Alcatraz. Adam Nordwall led a memorial powwow in San Francisco's wooded Stern Grove Park. Open to the public, it attracted more than a thousand people.

On Alcatraz itself, the Indians of All Tribes held quite a

different event to mark the anniversary of the takeover. At a news conference, attended by representatives of the media and the ninety or so current Indian occupiers, John Trudell and LaNada presented their plans for the development of the island. They displayed a model created by the San Francisco architecture firm of Donald McDonald. It consisted of a large ceremonial longhouse surrounded by other circular buildings to be used by the students attending the Thunderbird University to be established on the island.

Meanwhile, around the country, direct actions continued. That month, twenty-five Indian and Hispanic people, Grace Thorpe among them, scaled a chain-link fence and occupied an abandoned 640-acre former army communications center, about to be turned over to UC Davis. Their demand was that it be given to the Native and Hispanic communities for an ethnic studies center. Although the protestors were removed, UC Davis eventually withdrew its claim. The property ended up being used for D-Q University, a new two-year college devoted to Native American and Hispanic Studies, the initials D-Q standing for near-mythic figures from Native and Hispanic traditions. Founded in 1971, it was one of the first

LaNada Means and John Forster presenting an architectural model and blueprint for the creation of a "$6 million tuition-free university" on Alcatraz, November 21, 1970

six tribal colleges in the United States. Although it struggled financially and lost accreditation in 2005, gatherings, ceremonies, and powwows continued to be held on its grounds.

On Alcatraz itself, life was continuing despite the increasing difficulty of remaining on the island. More unexplained fires broke out, although all of them were quickly contained. The most notable one occurred in LaNada's own apartment. "I woke up," she said, "to see that the curtains were on fire. I was not thinking because I was half asleep and my first instinct was to protect my son. I threw myself at the fire and put it out with my hands. There had been a few other fires that same night and the guys were downstairs drinking coffee after battling another fire on the island. I lived over the dining hall. I emerged from my room, carrying my son downstairs with smoke following behind me. I handed Deynon off to someone and then fell over. My hands were badly burned and I went into shock."

Because there was no water available, they put her hands in milk. Then, because there would be no boat to the mainland until the next morning, she was settled for the night on a cot in the kitchen and guarded. Stella Leach sat by LaNada's bed all night.

At sunrise, wrapped in a Pendleton blanket her parents had given her, she walked outside, lifted her hands to the east, and prayed as the sun rose out of the bay. It was as if a message of reassurance was being given to her by the Creator. "I suddenly understood," she said, "and knew I would be all right."

When LaNada reached Dr. Tepper's office in Oakland the next day, he told her she had severe first-to-third-degree burns on both hands and she would never be able to use her fingers again. At best, the doctor believed, it would be at least a year before her hands even partially healed. "However," she said, "through my prayers I knew I would be okay."

She went back to Alcatraz the next day and, though there were traces of scarring, within a few weeks her hands had miraculously healed and she regained full use of all her fingers.

By early 1971, the number of people on the island had decreased considerably since that anniversary day when the optimistic plans for the island had been unveiled. Only a few dozen now remained. Grace Thorpe and her daughter Dagmar had left, at least in part because Grace had had enough of being criticized by others on the island who accused her of being more interested in seeing her father's Olympic medals returned than in supporting the occupation. Stella Leach, after numerous arguments with John Trudell, also returned to the mainland, immersing herself again in her nursing career and her advocacy for the health and well-being of Indian children. And, as had been the case in the past year, those occupiers who were students had returned to the mainland for their new semester.

LaNada, though, and John Trudell remained. Both were now on the island council. John was the recognized spokesperson while, often behind the scenes, LaNada was preparing press releases. For a time, they worked well together, but eventually a rift grew between them. Although Trudell had been on the island since the thanksgiving of 1969, he had never developed the connections in the Bay Area Indian community that characterized the earlier occupiers, and he was not a student. Suggestions made by LaNada were often vetoed by him. Because of his role as the voice of Radio Free Alcatraz, Trudell was now viewed nationally as the primary leader on the island while LaNada, still pursuing her studies toward a degree at Berkeley, had followed a much quieter path. John was much more concerned about his place as a national figure. When BANAC arranged for LaNada to go to Washington as their representative at a meeting, Trudell became angry. Then, as LaNada put it, he "cussed me out in front of everyone" because he thought of himself as the person who should have made the trip.

On April 19, yet another unexplained mishap occurred. *Clearwater* sank at its mooring alongside the island. Now there was no regular and dependable transportation to and from Alcatraz for the Indians of All Tribes. Some said it was not surprising. *Clearwater* was an old boat in need of repair. It just gave out. Others, though, felt it was a result of sabotage.

More and more people drifted away over the next months, until very few—among them LaNada and John Trudell—remained.

The federal government, meanwhile, had lost its patience. It had continued to keep the island under close observation. It became clear to the government that only a handful of people remained in residence at Alcatraz.

LaNada and a new group of Native students had been making plans to reoccupy the island. Their idea was to then proceed with litigation using a lawyer prepared to press their claims for the island to become a Native American university. The date to return was set for when school was out. LaNada's brother Dwayne would direct the Thunderbirds to remove anyone from the island who went against their efforts to hire the lawyer. The date set for their takeover and renewal of the occupation was June 12, 1971. Boats had been arranged and dozens of Indian college students had made their plans and packed their bags.

However, they did not know that a meeting had taken place at the White House on June 7. A major concern of the meeting was that the dark lighthouse on Alcatraz, unlit since the fuel for the generators had run out, posed a threat to navigation in the bay. In January, a Chevron tanker had narrowly avoided a potentially disastrous collision. It was also reported that intelligence showed there were only fifteen Indians left on Alcatraz. Throughout the occupation, President Nixon had been adamant that ending the occupation by force would not be allowed as long as public sentiment was in favor of the Indians. But now it seemed that public sentiment had changed and the small number of Indians still left made it likely that there would be little or no resistance. A meeting was held in Washington that included Undersecretary of the Interior James Beggs, Admiral Chester Bender of the Coast Guard, Deputy Attorney General Kleindienst, and members of the president's staff. It produced a memo listing a number of concerns.

> Aside from the continuing trespass, the intentional destruction of property, and the general lawlessness of the group on the island the lack of proper navigational aids leaves the federal government open to a possible negligence action should another maritime disaster occur.
>
> The Alcatraz takeover has continued to be an open wound, one that has become a symbol of different things to different people.

It was decided that acting immediately was not just necessary but politically expedient. It would afford time for any bad publicity to fade from public memory, because of the "long interval of time between now and the next election." When the memo reached the desk of John Ehrlichman, Nixon's primary advisor, his response was a simple one: "Go."

The students planning to bolster the Alcatraz occupation

also did not know that someone, whose identity remains unknown, had leaked their reoccupation date to the government. So it was, that on June 11, the day before the planned reinvasion, the Coast Guard sealed off the island. Thirty armed federal agents landed from three boats and one helicopter. In less than an hour, they had located and placed under arrest all fifteen remaining members of the occupation force. None of the six men, four women, and five children resisted. As a result, no one was handcuffed and restrained in any way. They were simply escorted to the pier and loaded with their personal effects onto the Coast Guard cutter *Point Heyer*.

Coast Guard Cutter removing last occupiers, June 11, 1971

They were taken first to Yerba Buena Island. There they were questioned, fed lunch, and then transported to San Francisco, where they were released and given a free night's lodging at the Senator Hotel in the Tenderloin district of the city. None of them had been in the original

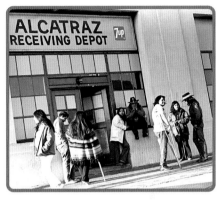

Occupiers stand outside the Alcatraz Receiving Depot. Right: John Trudell (Santee Sioux) and Amelia Anderson, Sitting: Harold Patty (Paiute), June 11, 1971.

invasion group on November 20, 1969. Both John Trudell and LaNada Means had been transacting business on the mainland. It's likely that the federal authorities, who'd been keeping Alcatraz under close surveillance, knew this and assumed there would be less chance of resistance with those two leaders absent. Trudell met them at the docks and went with the occupation force to the Senator Hotel and spoke to the press.

On the Monday after they retook Alcatraz, the federal authorities opened the island for a media tour. Newspaper accounts described its devastated appearance. Windows were shattered and buildings had been burned or partially taken apart for firewood. "Coiling along the narrow roads, looking like old skins shed by numerous snakes, were links of lead pipe dug up from utility tunnels, split and looted of their valuable copper tubing," reported the *San Francisco Chronicle*.

The government then proceeded to make Alcatraz even more unlivable for any group of Indians daring to invade again. The two apartment buildings on the lower level of the island were demolished. A chain-link fence was erected and guards with dogs were stationed on the island.

To some, it was a conclusion that seemed much like those lines from T. S. Eliot's poem "The Hollow Men":

> This is the way the world ends
> Not with a bang but a whimper.

Reporters who'd idealized the original occupiers now described the whole endeavor as a dismal failure.

But that was a shortsighted conclusion.

CHAPTER 14

WAVES AFTER ALCATRAZ

The ripple started by Alcatraz became a wave that swept across the continent. Dozens of other occupations took place over the next years, and at all of them the Indian occupiers cited Alcatraz as their inspiration. Organizing was still being done in the name of Indians of All Tribes, and in the years that followed many of those people involved at Alcatraz went on to be successful leaders and activists in Native causes.

Richard Oakes, Annie, and the children traveled back east to Akwesasne, where he met with members of the White Roots of Peace. Too weak to go back to ironwork, Richard and his family returned to California a few weeks later, where he was recruited by the Pomo Tribe to help in the fall of 1970 with their occupations of traditional Pomo land held by such corporations as Pacific Gas and Electric. Despite the fact that he was still weak and sometimes found it hard to walk, by New Year's Day of 1971, Richard had been involved in dozens of occupations in Washington and Oregon. This went on throughout the rest of 1971 and the first eight months of 1972.

On September 18, 1972, Richard was assassinated near the Pomo Reservation by a white caretaker who had earlier threatened his life. Like Martin Luther King, Jr., Richard Oakes's politics and national fame made him a target, and he lost his life to a racist. The outrage over the acquittal by an all-white jury of Richard's killer—who testified that Oakes had "lunged at him"—led directly to a Native march on Washington known as the Trail of Broken Treaties.

LaNada War Jack, who changed her name after Alcatraz to honor her tribal ancestor who was one of the great leaders of the Bannock, graduated from the University of California with an independent major in Native American law and politics. She went on to study at Idaho State University, where she obtained a master's degree in public administration and, in 1999, a doctor of arts degree in political science. She has taught at such schools as Idaho State University, Haskell Indian Nations University, and Boise State University. Over the years, she has held numerous offices in service to her tribes, including that of tribal chairperson of the Shoshone Bannock. Her activism continues to the present day. In 2018, she joined the Water Keepers, who were attempting to stop the potentially disastrous construction of an oil pipeline through the Standing Rock Indian Reservation in North Dakota. Her book *Native Resistance: An Intergenerational Fight for Survival and Life* was published in 2019.

John Trudell's involvement with Alcatraz was the beginning of a long career of activism. He would serve as the national chairman of AIM from 1973 to 1979 and also gain fame as a performance poet, reading his poems to the accompaniment of traditional Native music. His life after Alcatraz was not without tragedy, though. After divorcing his wife, Finicia Ordonez, who was with him on Alcatraz, he married Tina Manning, an activist of the Shoshone Paiute Tribe in 1972. They had three children together. Seven years later, while Trudell was burning an American flag at

John Trudell and other occupiers at the press conference in the Senator Hotel on Ellis St. in San Francisco, June 11, 1971.

a demonstration in Washington, D.C., a fire of mysterious origin swept through their house on the Shoshone Paiute Reservation in Nevada. Tina, who was pregnant at the time, her mother, and the children all died in the blaze. It is suspected to this day that Trudell's family was assassinated by the government. The FBI file bearing his name is seventeen thousand pages long. *Trudell*, a documentary film about his life, was released in 2005.

Grace Thorpe continued to be involved in Native causes after Alcatraz. Not only did she finally gain the return of her late father's Olympic medals and see his records put back into the annals of the Olympic games, but she also led a national movement that successfully prevented the storage of nuclear waste on Indian reservations.

Adam Nordwall remained active in Bay Area Native affairs for several years after Alcatraz. He taught Native American studies at Cal State Hayward for a time. In September 1973, ever the showman, while on his way to a conference, he came off the plane in Rome, Italy, dressed in full regalia, claimed the country by right of discovery, and then met with the Pope. That same year, he was given the name Fortunate Eagle and fully adopted by George Old Elk into the Whistling Water Clan in recognition of work he had done helping the Crow Nation. His time in the Bay Area came to an end shortly after that when his pest control business was fined for environmental code violations and he was audited by the IRS for underpayment of taxes, charges that held little merit but resulted in his filing for bankruptcy. Part of the reason this occurred was that Adam had been neglecting his business in favor of his activism. Some of his employees had taken advantage of this to embezzle from his company and do work that was slipshod and not up to code. But it was also Adam's well-justified belief that he'd been targeted by COINTELPRO for his work as an Indian activist.

Although he was invited back to his own Red Lake Reservation in Minnesota, there were few opportunities there for his family. Instead, in 1975, he moved with his wife and their children to her home on the Paiute Shoshone Reservation in Nevada. A successful artist who won awards for his sculpture, he was arrested and briefly jailed in 1987, charged with selling eagle feathers, but freed after the trial ended in a hung jury. He is the author of several books including *Alcatraz, Alcatraz* (1992), *Heart of the Rock* (2002), and *Pipestone: My Life in an Indian Boarding School* (2010).

As Adam Nordwall and other chroniclers of the Indian invasion of Alcatraz would note in articles and books over the years that followed, the Indian takeover of the island turned out to be one of the most consequential events for Native Americans in the twentieth century. As Benayshe-Ba-Equay, one of Adam's granddaughters, told me in an interview in 2022, "Alcatraz created a renewed sense of identity and hope after all the centuries of erasure."

She then went on to point out the results of twenty-six other occupations that followed: the founding of D-Q University; the creation of the Daybreak Star Cultural Center in Seattle after the 1970 takeover of the Fort Lawton military base that had been declared surplus by the Department of Defense; and the long, long list of successful presidential initiatives and Congressional Enactments benefitting Indians after President Nixon's eloquent message to Congress on July 8, 1970.

Alcatraz Occupier Atha Rider Whitemankiller (Cherokee) stands tall before the press at the Senator Hotel, June 11, 1971.

That list included the Self-Determination Act, the end of the termination policy, the return to Taos Pueblo of Blue Lake, the Indian Health Care Improvement Act, and the creation of the Office of the Assistant Secretary of Indians Affairs. Mount Adams was restored to the Yakima Tribe, Menominee termination was reversed and their reservation restored, assistance to urban Indians was increased, and the Alaska Native Claims Settlement Act was made law.

OF ALL TRIBES

Without Alcatraz drawing such wide attention to Indian causes and changing the public image of Native Americans, would all of that have been possible?

———

Today, Alcatraz remains a part of the National Park Service. More than a million visitors take the ferry to the island every year. Many of those visitors are Native Americans, who see the island as an inspiration and a shrine. The Park has now embraced the occupation by the Indians of All Tribes as part of its history. Slogans painted by the Native occupiers have been preserved or repainted. The former "Indian Land" is still a focus for Native American campaigns and nation-wide protests, including an "Un-Thanksgiving Day" on the island every November.

Numerous books about the events of those nineteen months have appeared, as well as such documentary films as *Taking Alcatraz*, *We Hold the Rock*, and *Alcatraz Is Not an Island*.

The words spoken by Richard Oakes in one of those documentaries remain true to this day. "Alcatraz," he said, "is not an island. It's an idea."

Ceremony on Alcatraz before the Long Walk for Survival from Sacramento to Washington, D.C., 1980, one of numerous events using Alcatraz as a symbolic staging ground

209

Indian kids playing below the lighthouse

SELECT ALCATRAZ TIMELINE

MORE THAN TEN THOUSAND YEARS AGO TO PRESENT: Alcatraz Island is part of the Ramaytush Yelamu homeland that encompasses the area around San Francisco Bay.

1493: Papal bull justifies Christian Europeans taking the Indigenous lands of the entire western hemisphere.

1500: California Indian population estimated at three to five hundred thousand.

1542–1769: Period of Spanish exploration of California.

1760–1821: Period of Spanish colonialism. Brutal Mission system decimates Native population. By 1821, Indian population is estimated at fifty thousand.

SELECT ALCATRAZ TIMELINE

1775: Spanish explorer Juan Manuel de Ayala gives the island its name, Las Islas de los Alcatraces, later Anglicized to Alcatraz. Although often translated as Island of the Pelicans, its literal meaning is Island of the Divers.

1778: First treaty between an Indian Nation and the United States is signed with the Delaware Tribe. Between 1778 and 1868, when the Treaty of Fort Laramie is signed, 368 treaties are signed between the United States and various Indigenous nations. All are eventually broken by the United States.

1803: Purchase of the Louisiana Territory from France, followed by the Lewis and Clark Expedition, beginning the U.S. exploration and conquest of the West.

1830: Indian Removal Act is signed into law by President Andrew Jackson.

1821–1848: Mexico gains independence from Spain, and California is part of Mexico.

1846: Alcatraz Island is purchased by John C. Fremont, the military governor of California for the United States. U.S. government eventually takes control of the island.

SELECT ALCATRAZ TIMELINE

1848: On January 24, gold is discovered in California.

1848: California becomes part of the United States.

1850: A ring of fortifications on and around the San Francisco Bay is designed with Alcatraz as a key point, and the island is set aside as a military reservation.

1851: California becomes a state.

1853: First lighthouse on the California coast is completed on Alcatraz Island, featuring a lens imported from France.

1858: First fort on the island is completed, with one hundred cannons and a garrison of two hundred soldiers. Fort Alcatraz begins to accept military prisoners soon after its completion.

1861–1865: American Civil War. Many Alcatraz prisoners are Confederate sympathizers and other Americans accused of treason.

1863: Building of the formal prison begins.

1873: On June 5, the first Indian prisoner, Paiute Jim, is transferred from Camp McDermit in Nevada. Two days after his arrival, he is shot and killed by a guard. Between 1873 and

1895, thirty-two Native Americans from various tribes are imprisoned on Alcatraz.

1879: Opening of Carlisle Indian Industrial School in Carlisle, Pennsylvania, one of the first of 350 such government boarding schools in the United States. Twelve thousand Indian students enrolled between 1879 and the school's closure in 1909. Between 1879 and 1978, more than 150,000 Native students were sent to boarding schools.

1881: *A Century of Dishonor* by Helen Hunt Jackson is published.

1886: Surrender of Geronimo marks the end of the so-called Indian Wars.

1886: The Dawes Act produces the allotment policy, resulting in immense losses of tribal lands.

1889: Oklahoma Land Rush.

1894: Largest group of Native Americans are confined on the island: nineteen "Moqui (Hopi) hostiles."

1900: Indian population of California estimated at ten thousand.

SELECT ALCATRAZ TIMELINE

1907: Alcatraz becomes solely a military prison.

1912: New, larger concrete prison is built on the island.

1933: Military ends its relationship with Alcatraz. Jurisdiction over the island is transferred to the Federal Bureau of Prisons.

1953: Termination policy orders the disbanding of more than 170 Native tribes and bands, terminating treaty rights.

1956: Indian Relocation Act sends tens of thousands of Native Americans to large cities for "job training."

1963: Alcatraz prison's final closure.

MARCH 8, 1964: A group of forty Native Americans, led by several Lakotas, briefly land on Alcatraz to symbolically claim it as Indian land.

1968: American Indian Movement (AIM) is founded in Minneapolis.

1969: More than twenty thousand Native Americans from more than one hundred tribes are living in the San Francisco Bay Area.

SELECT ALCATRAZ TIMELINE

OCTOBER 10, 1969: San Francisco American Indian Center burns down. It moves to a new location.

NOVEMBER 9, 1969: First attempt to take Alcatraz by the Indians of All Tribes.

NOVEMBER 20, 1969: Successful takeover of Alcatraz by Indians of All Tribes. Richard Oakes is the most eloquent and visible spokesperson.

NOVEMBER 25, 1969: A symbolic thanksgiving feast is held on the island with food donated from Bay Area restaurants and individuals.

JANUARY 5, 1970: Thirteen-year-old Yvonne Oakes suffers a fatal fall from the top of a flight of concrete stairs at Alcatraz. Richard Oakes and his wife, Annie, never return to reside on the island.

MARCH 1970: Alcatraz occupiers reject plans to make the island a "Native American Park."

MAY 1970: Water barge is towed away from the island. Phone service and electricity are cut.

SELECT ALCATRAZ TIMELINE

JUNE 1, 1970: Fire of a suspicious origin breaks out on the island, burns out of control, and destroys a number of buildings.

JUNE 11, 1970: While in Warren's Bar, Richard Oakes is attacked from behind by a Samoan man who had previously had a fight with him.

JULY 6, 1971: D-Q University begins offering classes. Grace Thorpe, who taught at the new tribal college, commented that "our getting this school will be a revival for us" and that "we need to instill confidence and pride in our people, to make them want to learn. So many feel that this isn't their country, as if they were foreigners in their own land."

JULY 8, 1970: President Richard Nixon's historic proclamation of the end of the policies of termination and relocation. Nixon's administration also returns substantial amounts of land to numerous Native nations.

NOVEMBER 1970: Twenty-five or more Indian and Hispanic people, Grace Thorpe among them, scale a chain-link fence and occupy an abandoned 640-acre former army communications center, about to be turned over to UC Davis. They demand it be given to the Native and Hispanic communities for an ethnic studies center.

APRIL 19, 1971: *Clearwater* sinks at its mooring alongside the island.

JUNE 11, 1971: U.S. government reclaims Alcatraz Island and removes the last fifteen remaining Indians.

SEPTEMBER 1972: Richard Oakes is shot and killed by a white camp caretaker in California, who is tried for murder and found innocent by an all-white jury.

OCTOBER 1972: Trail of Broken Treaties March begins, led by eight national Indian organizations galvanized and outraged by Richard Oakes's death.

1972: American Indian Movement occupies the village of Wounded Knee.

AUTHOR'S NOTE

In the fall of 1969, I returned to the United States after three years of volunteer teaching in Ghana, West Africa. In many ways—as an American Indian myself—I felt I'd come back to a country different from the one I'd left behind after graduating from Syracuse University with a master's degree. That feeling was due to the surge of Indian activism and awareness that became internationally visible through the Alcatraz takeover. It included not only the occupation of Alcatraz but also a number of things all happening around that same time, such as N. Scott Momaday, a Kiowa author, winning the Pulitzer Prize for his novel *House Made of Dawn*; the founding of the activist Native newspaper *Akwesasne Notes*; and the birth in Minneapolis of the

American Indian Movement (AIM)—things signaling what might be described as the rebirth of our Native nations. Hundreds of tribes that had once seemed doomed by federal policies such as termination began having their voices heard, taking control of the education of their children, and regaining sovereignty and sacred lands.

Although I did not take part in the Alcatraz takeover, many people I knew personally—such as Peter Blue Cloud and Grace Thorpe, both credited in my acknowledgments—played important roles during those complicated nineteenth months. I felt connected. But, then again, it's not an exaggeration to say that most Native Americans—even if they did not make the pilgrimage to Alcatraz—felt and still feel connected to that inspiring occupation.

However, it would be much later, looking back, that I would realize just how pivotal the invasion of Alcatraz by the Indians of All Tribes truly was in American history. It ushered in a new age of effective activism, often by people who described themselves as members of the Indians of All Tribes. The groundbreaking policies put into place by the Nixon administration were certainly influenced by the

AUTHOR'S NOTE

Alcatraz occupation and have deeply affected the lives of every American Indian to this day.

If you are not Native American or are not usually aware of recent Native history, the story of Alcatraz and its true importance is probably unknown to you. That is unfortunate, especially in the case of young people, who will carry the future on their shoulders.

There is a saying among the Lakota, one shared with me by my friend Kevin Locke, a traditional Lakota storyteller, flute player, and hoop dancer: "Take courage from the story."

The story of the Indian occupation of a small, rocky island that had been a symbol of despair but became a beacon of hope is something young readers deserve to know and take courage from.

And that is why I have written this book.

NOTES

1.

OHLONE LAND

4   "Although there is little doubt . . .": e-mail from Malcom Margolin, April 12, 2022.

6   "The Indians of California . . .": Elias Castillo, *A Cross of Thorns: The Enslavement of California's Indians by the Spanish Mission* (Fresno, CA: Craven Street, 2015), 52.

7   "California Indians were highly . . .": Rupert Costo and Jeannette Henry Costo, eds., *The Missions of California: A Legacy of Genocide* (San Francisco, CA: Indian Historian Press, 1987), 34–36.

10   "Among her own Pomo people . . .": Adam Fortunate Eagle, *Heart of the Rock: The Indian Invasion of Alcatraz* (Norman: University of Oklahoma Press, 2008), 158.

NOTES

3.

EXILED TO ALCATRAZ

21 "From 1873 to 1895 . . .": Gregory L. Wellman, *A History of Alcatraz Island, 1853–2008* (Mount Pleasant, SC: Arcadia Publishing, 2008), 21.

28 "The U.S. government's attempt . . .": Matthew Sakiestewa Gilbert, *Hopi Runners: Crossing the Terrain Between Indian and American* (Lawrence: University Press of Kansas, 2018), 54–59.

5.

CENTURIES OF DISHONOR

50–51 "the best thing that ever happened to me . . .": Phone interview with Adam Fortunate Eagle, March 14, 2022.

6.

THE LAKOTA LANDING

68 "Well, I guess if you want it . . .": Adam Fortunate Eagle, *Heart of*

the Rock: The Indian Invasion of Alcatraz (Norman: University of Oklahoma Press, 2008), 7.

7.

THREE ACTIVISTS

73   "I was always thinking of Alcatraz": Phone interview with Adam Fortunate Eagle, March 14, 2022.

74   "we were not forced as other kids . . .": Adam Fortunate Eagle, *Heart of the Rock: The Indian Invasion of Alcatraz* (Norman: University of Oklahoma Press, 2008), 19.

78   "Our tactic was to use . . .": Phone interview with Adam Fortunate Eagle, March 14, 2022.

79   "Bend down a second, Joe": Adam Fortunate Eagle, *Heart of the Rock: The Indian Invasion of Alcatraz* (Norman: University of Oklahoma Press, 2008), 54.

79   "Alcatraz is not an island . . .": ITVS documentary film *Alcatraz Is Not an Island*, itvs.org>films>alcatraz-is-not-an-island.

89   "I was a student and a mother . . .": Phone interview with LaNada War Jack, January 20, 2022.

NOTES

89 "were pillaged by both cavalry and immigrants": LaNada War Jack, *Native Resistance: An Intergenerational Fight for Survival and Life* (Virginia Beach, VA: Donning, 2019), 79.

92 "Before you start school . . .": LaNada War Jack, *Native Resistance: An Intergenerational Fight for Survival and Life* (Virginia Beach, VA: Donning, 2019), 115.

94 "I already knew the story . . .": LaNada War Jack, *Native Resistance: An Intergenerational Fight for Survival and Life* (Virginia Beach, VA: Donning, 2019), 127.

95 "try again another time": LaNada War Jack, *Native Resistance: An Intergenerational Fight for Survival and Life* (Virginia Beach, VA: Donning, 2019), 125.

95 "assimilate us and disenfranchise us. . . .": LaNada War Jack, *Native Resistance: An Intergenerational Fight for Survival and Life* (Virginia Beach, VA: Donning, 2019), 127.

8.

TAKING THE ROCK

104 "a vocational training center . . .": Adam Fortunate Eagle, *Alcatraz, Alcatraz: The Indian Occupation of 1969–1971* (Berkeley, CA: Heyday, 1992), 39.

NOTES

106–107 "We, the Native Americans . . .": Adam Fortunate Eagle, *Heart of the Rock: The Indian Invasion of Alcatraz* (Norman: University of Oklahoma Press, 2008), 207.

109 "Say, nobody's going to jump off . . .": Adam Fortunate Eagle, *Heart of the Rock: The Indian Invasion of Alcatraz* (Norman: University of Oklahoma Press, 2008), 79.

110 "to get the hell off the island": Adam Fortunate Eagle, *Heart of the Rock: The Indian Invasion of Alcatraz* (Norman: University of Oklahoma Press, 2008), 81.

112 "We landed at about 6 o'clock . . .": Kent Blansett, *A Journey to Freedom: Richard Oakes, Alcatraz, and the Red Power Movement* (New Haven, CT: Yale University Press, 2018), 130–31.

113 "What Indians? . . .": Adam Fortunate Eagle, *Heart of the Rock: The Indian Invasion of Alcatraz* (Norman: University of Oklahoma Press, 2008), 82.

113 "On the island, you can hide . . .": Adam Fortunate Eagle, *Heart of the Rock: The Indian Invasion of Alcatraz* (Norman: University of Oklahoma Press, 2008), 82–83.

113 "We could see them . . .": Adam Fortunate Eagle, *Heart of the Rock: The Indian Invasion of Alcatraz* (Norman: University of Oklahoma Press, 2008), 85.

NOTES

115　"We feel this so-called Alcatraz Island . . .": Adam Fortunate Eagle, *Heart of the Rock: The Indian Invasion of Alcatraz* (Norman: University of Oklahoma Press, 2008), 208.

118　"I heard about the occupation": Dean Chavers, "Alcatraz Is Not an Island," *World Literature Today* (Autumn 2019).

124　"Mayday! Mayday! . . .": Adam Fortunate Eagle, *Heart of the Rock: The Indian Invasion of Alcatraz* (Norman: University of Oklahoma Press, 2008), 101.

127　"People are going to get killed . . .": Phone interview with LaNada War Jack, January 20, 2022.

9.

A FIRST THANKSGIVING

133–134　"The island would host a center . . .": Kent Blansett, *A Journey to Freedom: Richard Oakes, Alcatraz, and the Red Power Movement* (New Haven, CT: Yale University Press, 2018), 132–33.

138　"a kind and gentle Choctaw woman . . .": Adam Fortunate Eagle, *Heart of the Rock: The Indian Invasion of Alcatraz* (Norman: University of Oklahoma Press, 2008), 134.

NOTES

10.

THOSE WHO CAME

144   "Dear America, the people . . .": Indians of All Tribes, *Alcatraz Is Not an Island*, ed. Peter Blue Cloud Berkeley, CA: (Wingbow Press, 1972), 1.

146   "published more than 125 articles about Alcatraz": *You Are Now On Indian Land, The American Indian Occupation of Alcatraz Island, California, 1969* (Los Angeles, CA: Twenty-First Century Books, 2011), 87.

157   "You guys did a good job . . .": Kent Blansett, *A Journey to Freedom: Richard Oakes, Alcatraz, and the Red Power Movement* (New Haven, CT: Yale University Press, 2018), 151.

157–158 "I would hitchhike off the docks . . .": LaNada War Jack, *Native Resistance: An Intergenerational Fight for Survival and Life* (Virginia Beach, VA: Donning, 2019), 150.

11.

AFTER THE FALL

166   "nothing was going right": Kent Blansett, *A Journey to Freedom: Richard Oakes, Alcatraz, and the Red Power Movement* (New Haven, CT: Yale University Press, 2018), 163.

NOTES

166   "You guys...": Kent Blansett, *A Journey to Freedom: Richard Oakes, Alcatraz, and the Red Power Movement* (New Haven, CT: Yale University Press, 2018), 169.

167   "the Indian biker gang without bikes...": LaNada War Jack, *Native Resistance: An Intergenerational Fight for Survival and Life* (Virginia Beach, VA: Donning, 2019), 176.

170–171 "All we get out...": Margaret J. Goldstein, *You Are Now on Indian Land, The American Indian Occupation of Alcatraz Island, California, 1969* (Los Angeles, CA: Twenty-First Century Books, 2011), 100.

172   "We announce on behalf...": Margaret J. Goldstein, *You Are Now on Indian Land, The American Indian Occupation of Alcatraz Island, California, 1969* (Los Angeles, CA: Twenty-First Century Books, 2011), 103.

12.

NIXON'S CHIEF

178   "He drilled into me...": Dr. Dean Chavers, "Richard Nixon's Indian Mentor," *Indian Country Today*, April 10, 2016.

182   "If we'd had guns...": Phone interview with LaNada War Jack, January 20, 2022.

NOTES

13.

TAKING IT BACK

188 "And now, with one . . .": Earl Caldwell, "Alcatraz Indians Short of Water," *New York Times*, August 16, 1970.

192 "I woke up . . .": LaNada War Jack, *Native Resistance: An Intergenerational Fight for Survival and Life* (Virginia Beach, VA: Donning, 2019), 166–67.

193 "I suddenly understood . . ." LaNada War Jack, *Native Resistance: An Intergenerational Fight for Survival and Life* (Virginia Beach, VA: Donning, 2019), 166–67.

195 "cussed me out . . .": LaNada War Jack, *Native Resistance: An Intergenerational Fight for Survival and Life* (Virginia Beach, VA: Donning, 2019), 172.

200 "Coiling along the narrow roads . . .": Adam Fortunate Eagle, *Heart of the Rock: The Indian Invasion of Alcatraz* (Norman: University of Oklahoma Press, 2008), 201.

BIBLIOGRAPHY

AP News. "Survivor of Alcatraz Escape Attempt Dies in Prison."
AP NEWS. October 5, 1988. See apnews.com/article/
f69748b0124a0f3ab629c9f0e7d65bc4.

Blansett, Kent. *Journey to Freedom: Richard Oakes, Alcatraz, and the
Red Power Movement*. New Haven, CT: Yale University Press, 2018.

Bowen, Peter and Brooks Townes. *The Sausalito-Indian Navy*. Weaver-
ville, NC: Peter Bowen and Brooks Townes, 1999.

Braun, Eric Mark. *Escape from Alcatraz: The Mystery of the Three Men
Who Escaped from The Rock*. North Mankato, MN: Capstone, 2008.

Caldwell, Earl. "Alcatraz Indians Short of Water." The *New York Times*,
August 16, 1970.

BIBLIOGRAPHY

Castillo, Elias. *A Cross of Thorns: The Enslavement of California's Indians by the Spanish Mission*. Fresno, CA: Craven Street, 2015.

"Carnes." *Salt Lake Tribune*. April 20, 1945, p. 7. See newspapers.com/clip/99976480/carnes.

Chavers, Dean. "Alcatraz Is Not an Island." *World Literature Today*, Autumn 2019.

------. "Richard Nixon's Indian Mentor." *Indian Country Today*, April 10, 2016.

"'Choctaw Kid' Carnes dies in prison." *Herald and Review*. October 6, 1988, p. 9. newspapers.com/clip/25810179/choctaw-kid-carnes-dies-in-prison

Costo, Rupert, and Jeannette Henry Costo. *The Missions of California: A Legacy of Genocide*. San Francisco, CA: Indian Historian Press, 1987.

Eargle, Dolan H., Jr. *The Earth Is Our Mother: A Guide to the Indians of California, Their Locales, and Historic Sites*. San Francisco, CA: Trees Company, 1986.

BIBLIOGRAPHY

Executed Today. "1948: Sam Shockley and Miran Thompson, for the Battle of Alcatraz." December 3, 2015. See executedtoday. com/2015/12/03/1948-sam-shockley-and-miran-thompson-for-the-battle-of-alcatraz.

Fortunate Eagle, Adam. *Alcatraz, Alcatraz: The Indian Occupation of 1969–1971*. Berkeley, CA: Heyday, 1992.

------. *Heart of the Rock: The Indian Invasion of Alcatraz*. Norman: University of Oklahoma Press, 2008.

------. Phone interview with the author. March 14, 2022.

Gilbert, Matthew Sakiestewa. *Hopi Runners: Crossing the Terrain Between Indian and American*. Lawrence: University Press of Kansas, 2018.

Goldstein, Margaret J. *You Are Now on Indian Land: The American Indian Occupation of Alcatraz Island, California, 1969*. Los Angeles, CA: Twenty-First Century Books, 2011.

Indians of All Tribes. *Alcatraz Is Not an Island*. Edited by Peter Blue Cloud. Wingbow Press, 1972.

Johnson, Troy R. *The Occupation of Alcatraz Island: Indian Self-Determination and the Rise of Indian Activism*. Champaign-Urbana: University of Illinois Press, 1996.

------. *You Are on Indian Land: The American Indian Occupation of Alcatraz 1969–1971*. American Indian Studies Center, 1995.

Justia Law. "Shockley v. United States, 166 F.2d 704 (9th Cir. 1948)." 1948. See law.justia.com/cases/federal/appellate-courts/ F2/166/704/1475755.

Kennedy Center. "Tim Tingle." kennedy-center.org/artists/t/ta-tn/tim-tingle

Mankiller, Wilma. *Mankiller: A Chief and Her People*. New York, NY: St. Martin's, 1993.

Margolin, Malcolm. *The Ohlone Way: Indian Life in the San Francisco-Monterey Bay Area*. Berkeley, CA: Heyday, 1978.

Murphy, Claire Rudolf. *Children of Alcatraz: Growing Up on the Rock*. New York, NY: Walker Books, 2006.

Murphy, Shelley. "'Whitey' Bulger wished for 'peaceful death,' prison letters say." *Boston Globe*. November 29, 2018. See bostonglobe.com/ metro/2018/11/28/letters-from-prison-bulger-wished-for-peaceful-death/AIm3dGuVTLcngpUOFasaHP/story.html.

BIBLIOGRAPHY

National Park Service. "The Army and American Indian Prisoners." See nps.gov/articles/the-army-and-american-indian-prisoners.htm.

Ranalli, Ralph. "Whitey paid for Alcatraz inmate's funeral Bulger didn't forget 'Rock' pal." *Boston Herald.* January 19, 1998. See web.archive.org/web/20110813034737/http:/rope.wrko-am.fimc.net/bulger/herald1.pdf.

Ritchey, Romney M. "Carnes Psychiatric Report (1945)." July 27, 1945. Archived from on June 8, 2007. See notfrisco2.com/alcatraz/bios/carnes/npsy714.html.

Smith, Paul Chaat, and Robert Allen Warrior. *Like a Hurricane: The Indian Movement from Alcatraz to Wounded Knee.* New York, NY: New Press, 1996.

War Jack, LaNada. *Native Resistance: An Intergenerational Fight for Survival and Life.* Virginia Beach, VA: Donning, 2019.

------. Phone interview with the author. January 20, 2022.

Wellman, Gregory L. *A History of Alcatraz Island, 1853–2008.* Mount Pleasant, SC: Arcadia Publishing, 2008.

Indian girls in traditional dress at the thanksgiving event of November 25, 1969

PHOTOGRAPHY CREDITS

ACKNOWLEDGMENTS

The takeover of Alcatraz was an intergenerational effort, with many older members of the Native community taking part, supporting, and guiding the young American Indian people who made up the bulk of the occupying force. I mention that because when it comes to recognizing those who inspired and assisted me in creating this book, I have to refer to first the Elders of that period and then those of my own generation—women and men now in their seventies and eighties. If Richard Oakes had not been killed a few years after the occupation, he and I would be about the same age now. Many of those who taught and inspired him, such as the members of the White Roots of Peace and Ray Tehanetorens Fadden, also were

ACKNOWLEDGMENTS

teachers of mine and deeply influenced my own life. I must always give them credit for helping put my feet on the path I've been walking as a writer, a storyteller, and, to a much lesser degree, an activist.

Much of what I put into this book I spent decades both reading and learning directly about before I ever began to write this volume.

I knew for many years people who played important roles during the occupation. Peter Blue Cloud, for example, was a dear friend. It was my great good fortune to get to know Grace Thorpe while working on three books and a documentary film about her famous father.

When I began researching and writing *Of All Tribes*, rereading books already on my shelves about the takeover and finding new ones, there was no book more useful to me than Kent Blansett's brilliant biography of Richard, *A Journey to Freedom*. Kent's conversations with me and suggestions after reading my manuscript were invaluable.

In some ways, reading the things written over the past decades about the Indian takeover is like revisiting the movie *Rashomon*—with multiple points of view interpreting the same event differently. Kent, in particular, helped me in my attempt to balance out those varying remembrances and sort out fact from inaccuracy.

I have to gratefully acknowledge two of the surviving central figures—LaNada War Jack and Adam Fortunate Eagle. Ktsi wliwini—great thanks to them for the books they have written, for being gracious enough to allow me to interview them, and most of all for their deep, lifelong commitments to Native rights. In addition, I need to thank Benayshe-Ba-Equay Titus, Adam's granddaughter, for her help in sharing with me Adam's close review of my nearly final manuscript for *Of All Tribes*.

Adam ended *Alcatraz, Alcatraz*, his first book about the occupation, by mentioning that his granddaughter was born on the fifth anniversary of the takeover: "A new and special life, a new hope for the future." And although Benayshe is modest about her own work as a teacher and an activist, I believe that Richard was right on the mark, not only about her but also about all those in the new and coming generations of our Native nations. They truly are the new hope for the future. This book is for them—and for all the young people of whatever ethnic background who believe, as did the Indians of All Tribes, in peace, in justice, and in human rights.

ACKNOWLEDGMENTS

Two more people who were more than generous with their assistance in making this book better are Ilka Hartmann and Brooks Townes. Both played important roles during the occupation of Alcatraz. The striking photographs by Ilka and Brooks that we've included add more than just a visual counterpoint to the text. I wish I could have included many more of their artistic images. Additionally, Ilka and Brooks each reviewed the manuscript, corrected errors, offered first-hand information, and made helpful suggestions.

My editor, Howard Reeves, deserves more than a mere shout-out for his efforts on this book, which took—thanks in part to the pandemic—at least two years longer than we'd projected. Completing it would not have been possible without his work and that of Sara Sproull, assistant editor. I deeply appreciate their diligence, their competence—and their patience.

It would be hard to find a Native community that is not connected in some way to the events that took place on Alcatraz Island. So many from so many tribes were part of the takeover, visited, or stayed there during the one year, six months, and twenty-two days when it was a self-proclaimed

ACKNOWLEDGMENTS

independent entity. It's impossible to name them all, but they all deserve acknowledgment and thanks.

To this day, Alcatraz is a place of pilgrimage for Native people. With that in mind, I also must acknowledge and thank the National Park Service for continuing to recognize the importance of those events and respecting that history by making it a part of their interpretive talks, developing exhibits on the island, and allowing events to take place that memorialize what happened and continues to happen there.

Last of all, though perhaps I should have mentioned this first, I need to acknowledge and thank not only the indigenous people of the Bay area, but Alcatraz itself. Once a hill and then an island, it may have been the start of a sacred path in Raymatush traditions. In the twentieth century, it saw the start of a new path for the Native people of the United States, one that continues to lead toward change, toward healing and growth.

INDEX

Note: Page numbers in *italics* refer to illustrations.

INDEX

INDEX

245

INDEX